THE DEVELOPMENT OF PERSONALITY

The Development of Personality

BY

T. A. RATCLIFFE

M.A., M.B., D.P.M., D.C.H.

London

GEORGE ALLEN & UNWIN LTD

RUSKIN HOUSE · MUSEUM STREET

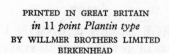

PRINTED IN GREAT BRITAIN
in 11 *point Plantin type*
BY WILLMER BROTHERS LIMITED
BIRKENHEAD

Author's Note

This book owes its origin, and part at least of its composition, to two main sources; to both of these I am indebted.

My chief debt is to Mr John H. Wallis. Mr Wallis is Training Officer to the National Marriage Guidance Council; and for a very long time I have worked in close advisory collaboration with him, and with that organization, in building up the basic and 'in-service' training programme for Marriage Guidance Counsellors. In the course of this collaboration we produced, both jointly and individually, a number of training booklets. As a logical, if considerable, forward step from this aspect of training, Mr Wallis suggested that there was scope for a book of much wider appeal and more detailed content. Although, therefore, this book appears under my sole name and authorship, Mr Wallis has contributed many valuable suggestions and comments during the process of writing it. I am most grateful to him both for his original concept of the book and for all his other help.

My other source of indebtedness is a much more indirect one. During the past fifteen years I have been privileged to conduct regular lecture courses on the general topics which this book covers at two universities, a school of occupational therapy, health visitor training courses and elsewhere. During the same period, I have been involved in numerous in-service training programmes for nurses, health visitors, teachers and social case-workers from many different types of agency. Since discussion sessions have formed an essential part of all these forms of teaching, I have been in the fortunate position of learning at first hand something of the value and limitations of social work (in the widest sense of these words); and a great deal about the problems which many students and workers find in relating theoretical training to the practical realities of their job. A major stimulus for writing this book was an attempt to answer some of the questions and problems which were raised with me during these various training sessions and discussions.

T.A.R.

Contents

Introduction

This book is written as an introduction and a practical approach to the basic ideas of modern dynamic psychology. It is intended as part of a programme of wider systematic reading. It has concentrated on these aspects of human growth and behaviour which are the direct and practical concern of those whose daily work brings them in contact with people in difficulty. Its aim is to relate theory to practical experience.

There are many excellent, authoritative text-books covering the theory of personality development and human behaviour according to the various specialized schools of psychology. But when one is faced with a client in difficulty or distress one cannot always understand the relationships between the client's problems and the theoretical concepts and theories. The social case-worker, the medical auxiliary, the clergyman, doctor, teacher, youth leader or (to say nothing of) parents, and many others need a bridge between theory and practice in their understanding of others. They do not confront their clients, or those seeking their help, under 'theoretical' conditions but under the stress and tension of the 'crisis' and the impact of a variety of immediate problems.

It seems to the author especially important that the reader should appreciate the relevance of these ideas not only to those whom he is trying to help, but to himself. The professional worker is just as human as his client; the parent or youth leader have the same basic reactions as those in their care. All have grown through the stages of development described in this book, with greater or lesser success. And that is, of course, equally true of the author!

The aim, therefore, has been to keep the following chapters as free as possible from theoretical terms and intellectualized concepts. This is not to insult the reader's intelligence, but because considerable experience of training students in many fields has convinced me that to be effective one must be intelligible at an empirical level.

All but the most superficial aspects of work with other people rests on an understanding of how our emotional development affects our ability to mature, to form relationships with others and the like. No one profession or vocation can claim a monopoly of interest in personality development. Nevertheless the contribution from psychology, psychiatry and the allied disciplines has added a new dimension to the age-old desire to understand our fellow-beings.

This short book is intended, therefore, not as a short-cut, still less as a substitute for further reading but as a stimulus towards it. An index or sub-divisions have not been provided because it is my hope that the book will be read as a whole, rather than used as a reference book.

Nor have I included a bibliography or made reference to more than an occasional book which has particular relevance to the text. It is likely that the student will be burdened already with a long reading list; and it would be no real help to other readers to provide what could only be an arbitrary selection from the many excellent books in this field.

CHAPTER I

The Earliest Years

A favourite theme with authors and playwrights is to take a group of people, subject them to some unexpected experience (a fire, flood, murder, accident, theft or pregnancy) and show how differently they react from one another. In the less dramatic surprises of life (off the stage) we notice similar differences. In any bus, railway compartment or aeroplane, individuals show wide variations in their reaction to delay, danger, inconvenience, interruption.

Even people we know well sometimes surprise us by reacting differently from how we ourselves respond. Although different audiences may laugh, cry or gasp at the same point night after night in the theatre, in daily life our reactions and responses are highly individual since we are not passive observers but are active participants.

Considering how different has been the life-experience of each one of us, this fact should not perhaps surprise us. We all have our own particular constitutional make-up, our own temperament, our own bodily differences. All these factors vary so much between individuals that we can seldom predict exactly how others will respond.

Nevertheless there are certain basic factors common to our developmental experience. There are stages of development that occur for all of us, even though the detailed ways in which we individually experience these stages will vary. In this book we shall be mainly concerned with the common pattern of experience as we develop towards maturity.

The process of maturation starts at birth. We are then independent only in a crude biological sense as a separate organism. At birth our capacities are very limited and we are entirely dependent on others for survival. Only as adults can we claim any real degree of independence, in the sense that we can 'stand on our own feet' (so far as that is possible in a complex society). How successfully each of us reaches a mature independence is fundamentally determined by our earliest experiences in the crucial first years of life.

The process of growing more mature is largely a matter of adapting our instinctual drives and desires to fit in with the needs of other people. For example, one drive is the desire to explore our surroundings. Without it we could never learn about the world we live in. We have to experience it if we are to learn what it is like. We cannot find our way through childhood, let alone establish adult standards, on hearsay evidence about our surroundings—of the difference between hot and cold, hard and soft, light and dark, nice and nasty, comfort and discomfort.

This vital process of exploring starts almost from birth. The infant learns to find the nipple, he gets 'the feel' of his own limbs, his toes, his fingers, the sound his rattle makes, the feel of his teething-ring, the water in his bath, mother's cheeks and nose and hair, the sound of her voice. At this stage his exploring can go ahead happily—though he may occasionally face frustration when he throws his rattle overboard and no one returns it.

As soon as he begins to crawl, his horizon widens and there is more to be explored. We cannot expect him to know that his drive to explore will now sometimes bring him into contact with what is dangerous or forbidden. When he encounters something new he will, as before, want to explore its feel, to taste it, to bang it on the floor, to hit it, to finger it. Quite inevitably some of his efforts must be frustrated. He must be removed from some objects (others must be removed from him) however exciting they may seem to him, and no matter how incapable he is of realizing why he (or the object) must be protected from his drive to explore, to experience. He cannot yet know that he is being protected for his own sake, to save him from getting hurt or from actual danger. All he can realize is that his compelling urge to explore is suddenly thwarted.

It is utterly unrealistic to suggest (as is sometimes done) that all frustration should be avoided. It is inevitable in almost every aspect of his early experience. We can see, too, (though he cannot) that to be frustrated and to learn how to adapt himself to it is an essential part of learning how to cope with life and therefore of character and personality development. How else can a child learn to come to terms with his instinctual drives on the one hand and the demands of his surroundings on the other? How else can he learn that, sometimes in his own interest and sometimes in the interest of other people, his own urges must be frustrated?

Yet this process is neither easy nor pleasant for him and it is unrealistic to expect that he will learn quickly and easily to tolerate frustration. And it is neither easy nor pleasant for the adults who care for him. Mother and child are both involved in this difficult task. A child of say three may want to have or to do something that his mother, quite rightly, cannot permit. His 'want' is both passionately expressed and urgent, as though his very life depends on getting his own way. He reacts in the same way as adults do when *their* urgent wants are forbidden—he gets angry. But he has not yet learnt adult ways of showing anger, by swearing or sulking, grumbling or banging the door or stomping off or taking it out on someone else. He therefore expresses his anger more dramatically and with less control, by what adults (rather loftily) call a temper tantrum. So far, this is a normal reaction. What happens next?

To his mother it feels anything but a normal reaction because she is so closely involved in his well-being. His uncontrolled outburst may be really frightening for her. Indeed, the more concerned she is for his welfare the more frightened she is likely to be. She may feel he is about to have a fit or injure himself by holding his breath or hurt himself by the violence of his kicks, the tenseness of his muscles, the intensity of his screams.

It is not surprising that the good, caring mother reacts urgently in an attempt to cut short this 'fit' as quickly as she can. She will be even more anxious to do this if the tantrum occurs in public, say on a bus or in a super-market. The disapproving looks of other people imply that she is a bad mother with an unmanagable child and add to her anxiety, making her feel it is her own fault.

With the best intention, a harassed and anxious mother is likely to take what seems to her the quickest way to end the tantrum. Since it began by her witholding something from the child (that is, frustrating him) the obvious remedy seems to be to give way to him. 'Oh, all right then, *have* it!' she says in her anxious exasperation.

Sometimes, of course, this is the expedient thing to do, for instance if she and the child are hemmed-in at a wedding, in the middle of the congregation, or if it is a long way till the next bus stop. But if an immediate giving way becomes a regular pattern the child soon learns that this is how to get his whims satisfied. He does not consciously think this out or make a plot but he learns, as it were intuitively, the sequence frustration-tantrum-satisfaction.

What matters more is that he is not learning one of the basic tasks of living—how to cope with frustration. His mother's reaction has enabled him to short-circuit this lesson. He begins to assume that his strong instinctive urges will be immediately satisfied provided they are expressed strongly enough. It then becomes increasingly difficult for him to begin the vital process of learning to fit in with the demands of his surroundings and the legitimate claims of other people. Instead, he will tend increasingly to be at the mercy of his own instinctive wants and urges. What began as a normal basic reaction to frustration can thus develop into a severe behaviour problem for this child or even a major failure of character development.

This mother's mistake does not arise from a failure of technique, in the sense of something prescribed for her by an outside authority. In a way (and as she sees the situation) she has reacted logically, at least in a short-term sense. Her mistake arises not because she is a bad mother but because she has not understood the importance of the lesson her child needs to learn from her. It arises also from an understandable lack of confidence on her part. Indeed, it has been said that to feel confidence in what one does with one's child is the most essential requirement in bringing him up towards maturity. This is largely true, though just to say so is not much help to the mother who lacks this confidence—it may even make her feel even more inadequate. What she needs is help with her anxiety, and a constructive rebuilding of her confidence.

The situation arising from the handling of a young child's temper tantrums is repeated in many other ways, both before and after the phase when these are quite frequent. It arises, for instance, in toilet training. In this, new demands are made on the child, new standards and a new regime are required of him and they involve a frustration of his strong instinctive urges. Why should he not continue in the old way, of getting immediate comfort or satisfaction? Again, his mother will be subject to considerable pressure—not so obviously from friends and neighbours, as happens later when temper tantrums begin. But the whole issue of being clean and dry is much coloured (whether she realizes it or not) by social taboos and conventions. And other mothers with small babies may claim a greater (or earlier) 'success' than she is achieving—not to mention her own mother and her mother-in-law, if these are to hand. If she is an earnest, well-intentioned mother she may develop an intense need to succeed with this training and she will become correspondingly vulnerable to evidence that her child is not up to some quite arbitrary standard. Many young mothers feel guilty and unsuccessful over this process as though they are facing the dead-line of some impending competition or some exhibition of dry and clean babies.

Our organs of excretion and of sex are anatomically such close neighbours that what might otherwise have been a simple process of learning new habits of hygiene becomes associated with intense feelings. Most young mothers do not realize quite how strong are their feelings about toilet training and it is easy for a prolonged and intense battle to develop between baby and mother. This may result in an anxiety to get him dry and clean as quickly as possible, or on the contrary to the reverse—when the mother abandons any attempt to train him, believing that it is bound to do him harm.

17

Weaning provides a somewhat similar situation between mother and child. The mother's anxiety is more openly felt. She is afraid her baby will suffer from malnutrition if he does not eat exactly the right amount of the right food. This too brings frustration for the child. Sucking is an easy, natural and pleasurable experience for him—a ready satisfaction of his instinctive need for food. Suddenly he is denied this easy satisfaction and immediate pleasure. A spoon is thrust into his mouth instead of the familiar nipple, solids instead of the easy flow of milk. The pleasant process of sucking no longer gets him what he wants. As at other crucial phases of the child's early development, his mother needs confidence but cannot always attain it. She has her own fears and anxieties about her baby's welfare and achievements and about her own attainments as a good mother, both in her own eyes and in the opinion of those around her. It is easy for a vicious circle to develop between mother and baby. Her anxiety increases the child's 'problem', this in turn increases her anxiety that she is failing him and that his well-being will suffer because of her. A calm and confident mother inspires her baby with calmness and confidence and enables him to weather the inevitable difficulties of development.

The adult's task is not to eliminate the child's instinctual drives and desires nor to play-down these vital forces. It is to enable the child to learn to modify them so as to fit in with the needs of others and to tolerate the inevitable frustration that this involves.

It is important that the degree of frustration to which a young child is subjected should not be too great for his age. It is unfair and unhelpful to demand standards appropriate to a child of six when he is only three. It is correspondingly helpful to his development if his mother can for the time being tolerate standards of behaviour that would not be acceptable in an older child, still less in an adult. This is the path by which he can learn to re-direct his strong inner urges and mould them into socially-acceptable patterns.

One can see this process at work as a small boy learns to express his strong feelings of aggression through fierce, ruthless and violent battles with toys or in brawls with his friends that are at once blood-thirsty and murderous, yet harmless and even friendly. If we adults can accept the validity of his powerful aggressive feelings and see them as potentially constructive we can help him to modify them and express them in acceptable ways. But if natural outlets are consistently denied him his basic aggressive drives will burst forth later in severe or anti-social ways.

Those who influence parents in handling young children have a special responsibility to realize the wide range of standards that are within the bounds of 'normal' behaviour. They should take into account the daily reality of the family and its standards and ways of behaviour, as well as the standards that can reasonably be expected of the children at any particular age. Unfortunately, a good deal of what passes for health education and an even greater proportion of professional advice given to parents fails to relate what is theoretically possible at each stage of the reality of the individual family and the special needs of individual mothers and children. Such advice may be theoretically correct, but irrelevant.

Unless advice is appropriate, in this sense, it may succeed only in provoking or increasing a sense of failure in the mother. She already has enough doubts of her own and she is subjected to many pressures as to what she ought to be achieving, what stage her child ought to have reached. Such pressures come upon her not only from educational and professional sources. Her natural anxiety is played-upon by commercial advertising. It is relentlessly suggested to her, either in words or pictorially, that she cannot be a good mother unless she uses such-and-such brand of detergent, soap or disinfectant, food, clothing or furnishing—or, in fact, almost any commodity that can possibly bear some relation to her role as mother.

Her desire to do the best for her child is a priceless asset in the complex task for which she may have had little or no preparation. But her very eagerness may defeat its own end, leading her to fuss and worry over relatively unimportant detail and attach exaggerated importance to more variations between her own baby and some hypothetical 'normal' child, so beloved of journalists and authors. The result is not unlike trying too hard to get to sleep early because of some important engagement next day—our attempts only serve to keep us wider awake, so that we bother about not sleeping as well as about the event that awaits us.

Far better than so much insistence on what is 'normal' for mother and baby, her advisers should foster the self-confidence of parents in handling their young children, giving more encouragement and understanding, and less criticism and doctrinaire advice. But it is, unfortunately, easier to pass-on expertise one has absorbed in a professional training than to keep one's feet realistically on the firm ground of family living, to be both knowledgeable and practical. Children react quickly to a parent's sense of failure and to weaknesses in child care. And so the doctor, health visitor, social worker or other professional person can greatly help a child by supporting and encouraging the mother. Many parents and in particular the rather anxious and meticulous parent need to be helped to understand how important is the task of saying 'No' when necessary; and that this does not produce for the child the automatic feeling that he has thereby lost the security of parental love.

It is equally important that parents should be able to say 'Yes' to their child and allow him what he can reasonably have or do, considering his age and the stage he has reached. Sometimes (although less often) parents need reassurance and guidance about this aspect of their caring. It is almost as easy to fall into the habit of prohibition, as in the old cartoon 'See what baby is doing and tell him not to', as it is to be afraid to say 'No'.

What most helps a child is a balance between granting and witholding, between approval and disapproval, so that he can learn to experiment, find his way in life and gradually discover what is permitted and what is not permitted. If he can thus experiment against a background of security and confidence, he will step by step learn to re-orientate his instinctive drives and desires and will learn the advantage of doing so.

Success in this vital process of learning (which begins

virtually from birth and continues right through childhood and even beyond) has far-reaching influences on personal development. Serious failures, if continued, gravely damage character development and seriously handicap the child throughout much of his later life. Success yields equally far-reaching gains in self-confidence and mature development. The most important factor is the quality of the relationship between the parents and the child. The two extremes of over-protection and over-demand can, and do, arise more from lack of confidence and understanding on the parents' part than from viciousness or stupidity. In the next two chapters we shall look more closely at variations in this primary relationship and the influence they have on the child's development towards independence and maturity.

Difficulties may arise not only from the parents themselves, however, but also from physical or intellectual handicap in the child. If, for example, his muscular co-ordination or development are faulty it will be correspondingly more difficult for him to learn simple movements which are the basis of more complex skills. If he is partly deaf or blind he cannot so easily communicate with others, if he has difficulty in running or playing he will not be able to fit-in so easily with the social rough-and-tumble of childhood games.

Such handicaps (particularly if slight) may for a while pass unnoticed. Sometimes parents and teachers are quicker to observe handicaps of sight or hearing than subtler difficulties of co-ordination. Moreover, it is probable that an infant relies initially on his sense of hearing, touch and smell and only later does he learn to use increasingly his more sophisticated senses. A defect of the more 'primitive' senses may be less easily observed; but it may be a greater handicap to the infant.

Other differences between the reactions of a young child and the adult must be considered if we are to appreciate all that his development entails. For instance, infants and young children are quick to sense or 'feel' an emotional atmosphere and do not (as adults *may* to some degree) reason it out or analyse the situation. Thus a child's emotional responses seem to pass through unaccountably quick and dramatic changes.

'But what is there to be afraid of?' we say to him, as though we can expect him to reason out some unexpected occurrence and its probable cause. His responses are immediate and intense. So is his sudden feeling of security when a trusted person comforts him, not with words and explanations so much as by action, by picking him up and cuddling him or taking him by the hand or stooping beside him and drying his tears. His fury, his terror, his tears, his laughter often seem excessive by adult standards and they often pass unaccountably quickly, as though, after all, they cannot have been real. Even when he has begun to talk he continues to express his strong feelings by action and gesture rather than in speech, dancing for joy, thumping with fury, stamping or throwing things about or jumping up and down in excitement. Similarly, he continues to be less influenced by the words of adults than by their actions, even when he has become quite fluent.

Earlier in this chapter we referred to the infant's exploring of his own body and his immediate surroundings. As he crawls and then toddles and plays with toys, he learns new skills of manipulations, of using his senses and his hands and limbs. These adventures bring new lessons for him emotionally, too —new kinds of joy and fun, gratification, frustration and fury, fear and adventure. Gradually his play takes on a new kind of learning, sharing his exploits and experiences with other children.

Each child of a group of three-year-olds has an absorbed way of playing, with little concern for what others are doing around them. Indeed, they seem quite unconcerned that other children are also playing, except when chance makes two of them both want the same toy. Even then, his reaction is more an expression of simple frustration than a response to the other child as a person.

A year later the same group play quite differently. Sudden rivalries still flare up but for much of the time the children are discovering new forms of co-operative play. In this active, practical fashion the four-year old learns the give-and-take of joint activity (that is of relationships) and begins to exchange his absorbed, self-centred play for activities shared with others.

In doing this he begins to develop an awareness of their needs. As he gets older he learns more of this critical lesson in both organized and spontaneous games. Presently he plays in quite sophisticated little groups, with a leader, a deputy and followers or 'other ranks'. With boys such groups often represent warlike, aggressive activities or adventurous exploring; with girls a replica of home or school with the leader as mother or teacher. Again an observant adult can see how children learn to 'act out' through play and phantasy some of their inner drives and urges, expressing feelings that cannot be fully expressed in ordinary life and living-through experiences in their imaginary world that would be forbidden or dangerous in reality. The adult (whether parent or professional worker) who understands these activities learns to comprehend the symbolic language of acting play and pretending through which our children are indirectly learning, sampling and experimenting with varying facets of life. They are thus learning to live, not learning about life at second-hand.

It is often stated that the child's first five years are crucial for future emotional and psychological development. True as it is, this observation must not be applied fatalistically, as though nothing significant can be achieved by parents or teachers (or anyone else) once a child is past his fifth birthday. Adults sometimes unthinkingly shrug their shoulders with a 'What can you expect?' when faced with the task of undoing some block in development which they correctly recognize as having originated very early in life. As with so much of our understanding of personality development, a sense of balance is needed if we are not to fall into unrealistic extremes.

It is certainly true that the foundations of personality are laid down in general terms by about the age of five and that early serious traumatic experiences can leave some mark on the later development of personality and character. Such foundations will, to a considerable extent, affect the strength of the personality-structure that is gradually built upon them. Nevertheless (as we shall see in later chapters) a great deal happens in later childhood and later life to modify the pattern;

and much can be done later to overcome these initial handicaps.

Similar criteria apply to the effects of inborn factors such as intelligence and type of physique. Many professional workers have observed from clinical experience that some children are much more vulnerable constitutionally to certain kinds of stress than to other kinds; or much more vulnerable than are other children. Behaviour is influenced by many different factors such as the stress of the actual situation, inborn constitutional qualities and earlier or childhood experience.

Personality development is thus another example of the old analogy of the soil and the seed. Whatever the inherent qualities in the seed, growth may be helped or hindered by the soil in which it germinates. But in the present context we should beware of thinking of 'soil' in purely physical or dietary terms. These are not ignored, but the vital soil for a growing personality is the emotional atmosphere, the quality of the relationships between the child and others around him and among the adults themselves among whom he is placed. One cannot adequately consider a child's development without taking these factors into account. He does not develop in isolation from others—indeed he cannot do so.

CHAPTER II

The First Relationships

However obvious it may be, we must emphasize that the early developmental processes described in the last chapter do not occur under laboratory conditions. On the contrary, they take place against a background of daily living which varies from family to family and from day to day. Whilst reader and writer are concerned with the infant, his instinctual drives and desires and the inevitable frustration he encounters, meals have to be cooked, the shopping done, father got off to work after his breakfast and all the countless routine tasks of running a home must be carried through, washing and washing-up, cleaning and dusting, things mended, tidied, discarded, shopping-list made, lost and found again, money counted, bills paid, letters read and answered, the rent man calls, the radio utters its daily fare of news and entertainment: a small world perhaps, but one that is full of noise and bustle. The baby is the most important concern but he is not the only one.

At the centre of it all there is no objective scientist or laboratory technician, calmly manipulating his apparatus until the lunch-hour, when he will find a meal awaiting him in the canteen. There is a mother who has perhaps been disturbed several times during the night by her baby, who is trying to deal with all these varied tasks at once and her baby, too. She will most certainly be subject to a host of frustrations such as we described as occurring to her baby. And she has her 'primitive instinctual urges' as well, sleep, rest, peace and quiet, her favourite activity (which may have nothing to do with household tasks or baby-minding) her favourite interests, her favourite radio programme. He is not the only one to have his urges frustrated. And he himself cannot avoid being part of his mother's problem, making great demands on her patience and energy, her ability to tolerate interruption and think of a dozen things at once.

Many a young mother in the throes of all this will smile a little wryly at our (very proper) emphasis on the importance of confidence in handling a baby. 'Confidence? she may exclaim. After a night like that and on a day like this? Where exactly do I get confidence from?' And any trim young social worker, visiting her on a Monday morning, should think twice before too readily entering in her notes as a devastating criticism 'Mother harassed, unconfident. Baby crying'.

A relentless drain on the morale of a young mother comes not so much from frustration, interruption or sheer hard work, but from the emotional demands to which she is subjected. A fretful baby may be exhausting not because of all the tasks its mother has to perform but for the opposite reason, that he is fretful in spite of them. She has perhaps 'tried everything' but he goes on crying. The implication of this to her may very well be that there is something 'wrong' with her, with the way she reacts to him, or something 'wrong' with him. If she has done all that the books and magazines and experts recommend and he still cries, then she can hardly help feeling the fault somehow lies in her. If a baby needs a confident mother, it is equally true to say that a mother needs a contented baby. But since a baby cannot read, books are written for adults, not for him.

The most important part of the baby's environment is not the noise and bustle, the warmth, the cot, the pram, important to him as these are. It is mother herself. The most perfect material conditions cannot make up for the handicap of a mother who basically does not want the child. Conversely, a baby who is basically wanted has the best possible start in life which far outweighs deficiencies in the amenities of the home. It is not a matter of what mother proclaims but of her real inner feelings. This is what determines the degree of security that a baby gets from his mother and it is something that is very difficult to replace.

He is so dependent and has so much to learn that he needs a great deal of security if he is to thrive and develop. It is therefore natural—indeed, desirable—that his feelings for mother and soon for father too, should be (by adult standards)

26

utterly possessive. We should not be surprised at the look of sheer panic that comes over him when mother for a moment covers her face with her hands or hides it behind a cushion—or at the delighted laughter with which he discovers that she is still with him.

To the small infant, the whole world consists of his own body and any object or person that comes into close contact with him. He regards these as extensions of himself. Thus his primary relationship to mother and father (the two people closest to him) is demanding, possessive and self-centred. He feels them to be *his*, as though they are a part of him. His relationship is a 'taking', not a giving relationship, even though they derive great pleasure from his very presence. Later (when he can sit up and when he begins to crawl or walk) he comes to recognize that a totally possessive and 'one-way' relationship cannot continue. He realizes that he shares mother with father, and him with her. And this discovery does not please him.

A momentous stage in his progress comes therefore when he first begins to recognize that mother is not exclusively his, is not a possession to be relied upon absolutely and unconditionally, to satisfy every want. His discovery of father is a critical step forward, out of the lost paradise of complete dependence and demand on mother.

Gradually this discovery unfolds into its next phase, the realization that he has two people who care for him and that they also care for one another. It is a great day for him when he takes his first few staggering steps from mother to father and then back again, sharing with each in turn his delighted triumph. The discovery (continually rediscovered throughout life) that relationships can be and must be shared is only in part a 'lost paradise'. It can also lead to a gain in confidence and freedom provided it occurs against a loving background. Many years later, this situation will be echoed in feelings of possessiveness and jealousy or in confidence and trust when he is married. The wife who feels threatened because she must share her husband with his other relationships at work, the husband who resents his wife's relationship to her parents, are examples of such echoes. The real meaning of the adults' predicament is to be found in the lack of loving care that should have supported them early in life when this first lesson had to be learned.

At this stage in his development the young child will naturally require and demand a great deal of attention. He will respond quickly to the discovery that father too can be a playmate and can cherish him. Then suddenly he may rush to mother or cling to her skirts, to be picked up. Quite often, too, he will try quite literally to come between his parents and separate them.

Throughout the crucial period between six months and three years of age, the infant tries to maintain a demanding and possessive relationship. To have to give this up is yet another frustration for him, which he does not want to accept. But if he is to develop and mature he must learn to cope with this as with other forms of frustration for it has vital implications for the future development of his character and personality.

As he becomes more fully aware of his parents as people, more vulnerable to their seeming sometimes not to care about him, he begins to make another far-reaching discovery. He becomes sensitive to their approval or disapproval. He discovers that demand is not the only way to get 'proof' of his parents' loving care. He can get their admiration and approval by his actions. He learns that what he does will bring a significant response from his parents. His parental relationship feels stronger when they are pleased with what he does and weakened when they disapprove. In some degree he confuses these responses with being loved or being not loved. Indeed, as adults we are perhaps never quite free of the same confusion, sometimes feeling not liked when someone important to us simply disagrees with an opinion or disapproves of an action of ours. Parents who successfully convey this distinction to their children, not so much by explanation but simply through understanding it themselves and continuing to show love, do them an important service in laying the foundations of social courage. And reformers with the courage of their convictions are still both rare and necessary.

The young child, then, quickly learns the rewards of pleasing his parents by what he does and the penalty of incurring their disapproval. He will try hard to do what pleases them, what is acceptable, so as to strengthen his relationship with them. But adult standards are often incomprehensible to him (as indeed they often are to other adults) and it will not be easy for him to be sure what will please them. He cannot easily understand that some behaviour may be acceptable sometimes but not always—for instance, if there are visitors present or in-laws in the room.

Soon he begins to pattern his behaviour on the parents' and especially on the parent of the same sex, as an extension of this same process of trying to be acceptable through his behaviour. If (by and large) mother and father are acceptable to each other, then obviously the way to please one of them is to act like the other. Of course it is not suggested that he reasons this out, but that is how he reacts to the problem of pleasing them—just as if he did reason it out in that way.

This process shows itself in everyday activity. The little girl bustling about with her dolls, dressing-up, doing housework, laying the table, preparing a meal—all in make-believe, shows unmistakably that she is 'being mother'. It is not only copying mother, as one may imitate a gesture or mannerism. It is more like an experienced actress who has 'absorbed' a part so fully that she spontaneously knows what mannerisms or gestures to use and, as we say, 'lives' the part and creates something that is in part what the playwright intended and in part something of herself. This is more than mimicry, and so it is with the little girl, absorbed in her dolls-house or playing with her toys.

Often a trained observer can get a vivid and accurate picture of what a mother is like as a housewife from the way her three-year old daughter plays at 'house'. And the little boy with his toy steering-wheel, banging on the wheel or ramming home the gears, may present an all-too-true caricature of his father's driving in unfavourable traffic conditions. A young child cannot easily distinguish between ways of behaving that actually are pleasing to the other parent from those which are irritating. This fact provides a certain amusing piquancy for the parents as they watch the apparently merciless exposure of some of their own less creditable actions. But it is not intended to be merciless, and the mother or father who indulges a little mild malice in pointing out that the child is 'just like' the partner at that moment may attribute calculated astuteness to a child who is merely observant and imitative.

Children sense very early in life which sex they are—that is to say, which parent they will 'copy' in the way we have been describing. In this way they not only learn how to please the parent of the other sex, they also form for themselves their first picture of masculinity or femininity. They are finding a pattern to follow, as though they say to themselves, 'This is what I shall be like when I'm grown up, this is how I shall behave, these are the things I shall do.' These patterns will be based partly on what the parents are actually like but mainly on how the child sees them. Parents expect their children to learn how to accept frustration but this will obviously not be so easy if the boy is modelling himself on a father who has never really learnt this lesson himself. No wonder most parents remember the quip 'Don't do as I do. Do as I say'. But it is not just a matter of the parent having to be a model of good behaviour for the child. The process of patterning is more subtle than this and children are not easily deceived. The parent who finds it very difficult to tolerate frustration has to learn how to, however late in the day; it is not enough to pretend he can, when his little boy is around. This only lays a foundation of inner confusion which may have quite serious results in later life. Perhaps we should add here that we are not trying to lay down the law about what parents should or should not do about this. Our aim is to foster a wider understanding of what actually happens and what consequences are likely to follow.

The young child's realization that his two parents fulfil different roles and that he will one day be like one of them carries with it the origin of his feelings about sex. But it is a mistake to attribute to him the fully developed sexual feelings that we know as adults. He cannot possibly know the full meaning of sexual feelings until after puberty; but we need also to avoid the other extreme of supposing that it is nonsense to use the word sex at all when we are talking of very young children. Obviously, even infants get feelings of pleasure from fingering parts of their body, including their sexual organs, and as we have been explaining, very young children do recognize differing functions of their two parents. Both are, so to speak, functions of infantile sexuality but at a different level of intensity from their equivalent in adults.

The little girl sees that father shares mother with her and sometimes she will resent it, wanting daddy to herself and trying to push mummy away or sometimes vice versa, but feeling left-out and resentful or jealous when they seem to want each other rather than her. A little boy will resent his possessiveness of mother being rivalled by father. Such feelings are basically sexual in the sense that they are differently felt towards the two parents and are associated with the fact that there are three people involved but only two sexes. This triangular situation has great personal significance in the child's development. It arises from two factors, the need to try to perpetuate an exclusive and possessive relationship with the parent of the opposite sex and secondly the fact that this relationship cannot be perpetuated but must be shared; that is to say, there is a rival of the same sex.

It may seem odd or far-fetched to speak in terms of sexual rivalry when we are considering a child of two or three, yet this little triangular drama is acted in the daily life of the family. Only if we think of sexual rivalry or jealousy exclusively in terms of adult sexual intercourse, will it seem absurd. Indeed, parents themselves, for all their sophistication and later development, are not immune to the emotional triangle involving themselves and their child. It is perfectly possible—and indeed quite usual—for a father to resent some of the care and attention his baby son commands from its mother, and for a wife, even while she laughs at herself, to pick up her little daughter off Daddy's knee a trifle sooner than she need. To some extent, no doubt, this is simple rivalry, unrelated to sex, and parents may feel some jealousy of their child, whichever sex it is. But there is also some sexual colouring as well, as can be seen when they have both a boy and a girl. A father may resent his wife paying a lot of attention to their son, but not to their daughter. He will perhaps argue that, after all, she must not make the boy effeminate. But he is not likely to find that his wife agrees with him. She in her turn will sometimes tell him that he must be careful not to 'spoil' their daughter by too much attention, but she sees the attention he gives their son as companionship.

Provided the parents' own sexual life, in both its narrow and its wider implications, is relatively satisfying, these domestic rivalries simply form part of the never-ending variety and interest of a growing family, at once both light-hearted and serious. But if either or both of them was never in their turn able to weather these early stages with adequate security and confidence, then quite intense difficulties may arise. If either parent has still a possessive and exclusive need to be loved, it will be correspondingly difficult to share the other with the new baby, particularly a baby of the same sex. Even though a mother's feeling towards her young son are not sexual in the ordinary adult sense, she may show an almost infantile possessiveness towards him. Similarly, a father handicapped in the same way by not having grown through his early triangular situation in childhood, may feel quite irrationally threatened by the presence of a rival for his wife's love. He may become very possessive of his little daughter or rejecting towards his son, although his feelings, also, are not sexual in the wholly adult sense. Indeed, it is precisely because husband or wife in these examples cannot be fully adult in their sexual relationship that such difficulties arise. And perhaps we should add here that being sexually adult implies much more than the ability to have sexual intercourse; it means being relatively mature emotionally as well as being sexually capable. But since this all-round maturity is the goal of personality development, it will be considered in later chapters.

Provided the sexual relationship, in the fuller sense, is relatively satisfactory, the young child and the parents will be able to share relationships within the family and later outside it also. Gradually the child builds up a composite picture of maleness and femaleness. One of these he is aiming at, the other he will see himself in relation with. He gradually forms his ideal of each sex, even though these rest on the original foundation of his two parents.

At about the stage we are considering, the parents may have a second child. Since (because of conventions of grammar) we have so far been calling the baby 'he', we will suppose that he now has a baby sister. So much has been written about this situation that it is all too easy to fall back on the expression 'sibling rivalry' to explain almost any difficulty that may arise. Difficulties are not helped simply by using labels (however accurate) but by understanding the full implications of what is happening. Any change in family structure so radical as having a second child is bound to influence the whole family, not only the first born. Let us, however, begin by looking at the event through his eyes.

Naturally and properly he has been the centre of the picture. He is the event of the family and friends and relatives have paid him the homage of their attention. He has obviously been the centre, too, of his parents' care and attention. Every day has brought some new item of importance springing from him, some new achievement, some new difficulty or upset. This is the world as he has known it, and only as he has known it. The cot is his, the pram is his, the toys are his, the home is (very largely) his, mother is his and father is his. He has seen other children outside his home, and for short times inside, but they have had no great significance for him. Just as important is the fact that they have had no great significance for mother either, just somebody else's baby.

Just when he is going through some of the important stages we have been considering, this shattering event occurs. Heralded by mother's sudden disappearance out of his immediate surroundings (if not into hospital) this new rival appears in his home. Nowadays parents are usually careful to let him know that a baby brother or sister is expected, so that in one sense the birth is not absolutely unforseen. But often they deliberately give him the impression that it will be a completely joyful innovation. They do this with the best intention,

33

believing that they can help him thus to see it in the same way, whereas in fact it may only add to his confusion and his disappointment. It is wiser to let him understand the bare fact, which is startling enough, and wait to see how he will view it. It is hardly fair or reasonable to pretend that it will be all fun for him. Indeed, he is lucky if it is any fun at all.

Parents are naturally proud of the new baby and mother's return to the family is a cause for rejoicing, the beginning of an exciting new chapter in the family's life. But to the first child it can hardly seem like this. Mother disappeared and he was left with some makeshift caring by father or a grandmother or a neighbour. Then she returns, bringing with her this new baby that everyone crowds around. She must naturally give it almost all her attention. Whoever was caring for *him* now goes back home and he is left with what care and attention mother and father can still spare him. But father is busy helping mother and she is busy with the new arrival. To crown it all, he is expected to be thrilled as they are, to admire his new sister, to be helpful and quiet and happy. If he does make any demand for attention he gets told not to be a nuisance, that he is a big boy now he has a baby sister. This is a poor exchange for the attention he used to get when he needed or demanded it, before this rival came on the scene.

How can this little boy possibly see the situation as his parents see it or as they want him to? The protests that he makes at mother's preoccupation with the baby are not just 'naughtiness' as she and her husband may feel they are. His demands for some return of the old care and attention that used to be lavished on him only add to her difficulties. She now has two young children to look after and it is easy for her to be cross with him and not understand how he is feeling. But this reaction endorses his conviction that he is no longer the centre of the family and that the cause is this new rival.

Nothing can alter the fact that his position as the focal point the family *has* been usurped and that mother must give a great deal of her time and attention to the new baby and much less to him. And it is certain that he will respond to this change. But if the parents can understand how he feels, they will be less likely to get impatient and cross with him or just write-off his distress as 'jealousy' which he could control if he wanted to.

He may react to this new development in many ways. They are not unlike the ways adults react to the same kind of change —when a new rival suddenly appears and usurps their former position, for instance in business or if a close friend or married partner shows a preference for someone else.

He may show an open hostility towards mother, getting angry with her and hitting her when she is feeding or bathing the baby or by knocking something over in a rage. Or he may direct this hostility at the rival by taking away her bottle or rattle or giving her a sly pinch or exclaiming 'Horrid baby!' at her or asking mother when she is taking the baby back.

He may express these feelings less openly and make a bid to regain the position he formerly held by demanding attention to himself in whatever way seems appropriate, by being hurt, tearful, unhappy, or finding a bump or bruise or ache or not getting to sleep or falling over. His bid for attention may take the form of being 'tiresome', constantly doing things that he knows mother will not ignore, for he would rather be scolded than ignored. It is at least a form of attention.

Sometimes he may deal with the rival in a different way by seeming to dispose of it, pretending it is not there after all, like the little boy who put the biggest cushion he could find on top of the baby while she was lying on the sofa before her six o'clock feed—a time when mother used to play with him. Such an action can seriously alarm parents, who may feel he is trying to smother the baby. But he is much more likely to be assuming that out of sight is out of mind and making an attempt to erase the rival from the family scene and thus regain the focal position that was his own.

Another way in which he may react is by reverting to babyish ways. He may start bed-wetting again or become unable to dress or feed himself or do simple tasks that he has been managing successfully. He may return to thumb-sucking and baby-talk or even to an inability to walk or talk at all, as though he was feeling that since a baby can capture the attention that was formerly his, the obvious thing to do is to return one-self to babyish ways.

But one must not assume this little boy works all this out in his head. It is most unlikely that he has any clear idea why he is behaving in these ways. The explanation of what he is doing is not much help to him, but it should help the parents to deal more effectively with his problem. And it is important for his future development that they should. As with his temper tantrums (which we referred to earlier) what he does is not so important as the way he is handled when he does it. If the parents can realize that his reactions make sense and are normal and are not simply 'naughtiness' or delinquent tenden-cies they will see what action on their part is appropriate. This will avoid a vicious-circle developing, in which their punish-ing reaction only confirms his feeling that he is not loved as he used to be. For instance, they may be able to find ways of recruiting his help with his baby sister at bath-time or ways of giving him some special attention all to himself when the baby is in the room, so that he can see for himself that the rival does not always have first claim. Lengthy explanations or just giving him lavish presents will not really help. He needs reassurance that he is still cherished, still important in his own right, even though the family has now changed its pattern. If this can be done successfully, he will gradually become adap-ted to the new situation and eventually recognize that there are advantages in being the eldest and in having a little sister in the family.

Sometimes this important stage in a family's development will pass with little disturbance or difficulty for anyone. Some-times quite serious problems arise. The difference does not lie in one factor alone. The way the parents deal with it is an important factor and so is the stage which the first child has reached when the new baby is born. This is not simply a matter of age but of how far he has already learnt that relation-ships have to be shared—particularly his relationship to mother—and how far he has learnt to deal with frustration. And his progress in these ways will depend on how far his parents have been able to help him, how they have handled him. And finally, his own in-born temperament and physical make-up will affect the issue too.

Although it may seem too obvious to require stressing, we are apt sometimes to ignore the fact that the primary relationships which we have described in this chapter, and indeed all normal human relationships, exist between real people. Now real people, whether they be children or parents, do not always act 'reasonably'. As we have already noted, parents are under considerable pressures arising both from within themselves and from the expectations which other people in their environment have (or seem to have) for them.

There can be few parents, therefore, who have not been unjustifiably cross with their child at some time or other; or, at the other extreme, given the child equally unjustified praise and credit. Provided such situations are not a regular or frequent pattern of the family's life, and that the basic relationships are good, such 'injustice', whilst it may cause temporary distress, does no real or lasting damage to the child—or to the relationship. But, understandably enough, most good parents will feel some sense of failure, or even guilt, over such an action. The danger here lies in the risk that this same sense of failure and guilt may spread equally to those occasions when the parents are justifiably cross with their child. It is easy for parents to see such annoyance and disapproval as the very negation of love. And there are few children who will not dramatize such a reaction as this to their own advantage. The child's counter-comment of 'You're horrid. You don't love me' or 'I'm going to run away from this horrid house' are as sure a way as any other through which he may manipulate himself out of further trouble!

It is important to stress, therefore, that the good, and genuinely loving, parent must be able to say 'no' as well as 'yes'; able to withhold as well as to give; able to show disapproval as well as approval, in each instance according to the needs of the child at that particular time. Only then will adult and child be able to see each other as 'real people'; only then will the relationship be fully loving, genuinely satisfying to both parent and child, and constructive in its results.

CHAPTER III

The Incomplete Family

In the previous chapter we considered stages and events which took place within the simplest complete family structure of two parents and their own child or children. There are obviously many possible variations in this pattern of family living; and we must also consider some of these differing situations and their implications for the child's development.

Some families have other adults living with them as well as the two parents. There may be one or two of the grandparents and the family may be living in *their* home or they in the young parents' home. Such differences must affect the environment of family life and thus the young child's experiences. Grandparents may play quite a large part in caring for and training the child, particularly if the mother goes out to work whole-time. But even when they give no such help their presence must modify the routine of the family and the parental attitudes towards each other and towards the child. Sometimes, too, there may be step-children in the family. And if the baby is born towards the end of a large family there may well be brothers and sisters who regularly 'mind the baby'.

Such differences can produce more far-reaching results than one might expect. As was stressed earlier, young children are sensitive to the emotional atmosphere in the family and respond quickly to changes in it. If the presence of Granny is welcomed or accepted this atmosphere will be very different for the young child from an atmosphere in which she is unwelcome or resented. The same is true of other people in the home.

Young children are quick to respond to changes of routine, but changes in his feeding and bathing routine will affect him differently according to whether these arise from welcome or unwelcome changes within the family, from whether the atmosphere gets more confident and easy or more tense and difficult in such circumstances. The arrival of a bereaved or sick grandparent into the family may be accepted with complicated mixed feeling by the parents; and the child will respond accordingly. It must be stressed, too, that the basic relationship between parents and grandparents is inevitably a complex one. After all the grandparents were *their* mother and father and neither side can wholly forget, or grow past, this fact.

Without minimizing in any way the significance of the various possible variations in family pattern described here, and later in the book, it will be clear from the facts described in Chapter II that the primary and most essential relationships for the child are with mother and father. Any loss of, or damage to, these relationships must produce difficulties, and sometimes grave and lasting damage to the child. Such parental relationships are of great importance at every stage of childhood and adolescence. The loss of a parent at any age must be distressing experience, and may, in certain circumstances, initiate deeper emotional damage as well as unhappiness. But it is during the first two or three years of life that the child is most vulnerable to, and more likely to be damaged by, the loss of a parent. We are especially concerned here therefore by the impact of such an 'incomplete' family on the development and security of the very young child.

It will be clear that there can be varying degrees of loss of such a relationship with the parent. Brief, or relatively short, separations may result from such factors as illness in parent or child, with the need for one or other to be away in hospital; or by the demands of the father's work or the mother's departure to look after a sick relative. At the other end of the scale there may be the complete and permanent loss of parent from death, or desertion or divorce. In all these circumstances mother or father is actually and physically absent. It must not be forgotten, however, that even when the parent is actually present 'in the flesh', he or she may still be the absent parent in every emotional sense. The unloving parent, the rejecting parent, or the parent who for one reason or another cannot be 'motherly' or 'fatherly' towards this particular child may be just as surely depriving the child of his needed primary relationship as if that parent were a hundred miles away. It is harder to realize, but nevertheless as true, that the too loving, the too anxious or the too protective parent may sometimes provoke some sense of deprivation and relationship loss for the child.

As we showed in the previous chapter, the infant's gradually increasing ability to rechannel his instinctual drives and create his standards and the foundations of his future personality and character, build up within, and essentially because of, the parent-child relationship.

Inevitably, therefore, any damage to that relationship must have repercussions in these areas. But this primary relationship is something more than this. It is the infant's first contact with another human being. Its pattern forms the foundation for all his future human relationship; and it provides the basic security which he desperately needs. No building can be erected properly on shaky foundations; and damage to the foundations of primary relationships must have its serious results on the child's (and later the adult's) ability to form secure, mature and stable relationships.

It is easier to study first the impact of parental loss in its simplest form—that of the absence of the father during part of those crucial first three years of the child's life.

At this stage of infancy the father is the less significant of the two parents. This is not to say that he is unimportant, although his significance has been much underestimated by some writers. But his status and role increases as the child grows older, and probably reaches its zenith with the adolescent son or daughter. What then *is* his role vis-à-vis the infant and what effects will his absence have?

Because he has to earn the family living, father cannot be there all the time. It is all the more important that he and his wife should realize how important is the part he *can* play in the child's development. If, when he gets back from work, he plays with the child or puts him to bed, or pushes the pram; if he remembers emotionally as well as intellectually that this is *his* child too, then his infant will come to see and feel him as a 'real person'. Unfortunately not all fathers get home early enough for such activities; and not all are prepared to build such a contact even if they do. Some fathers must be away from home for continuous periods and some have to work at weekends. To the extent that these limitations occur (and regardless of whether it is anybody's fault) we must regard the family as 'incomplete' and expect some consequent reaction.

So far as the young child is concerned, there is virtually no difference between a father who is miles away driving a lorry and one who is shut up in the next room writing a book or watching television. Or father may be actually in the room but so uninterested or so preoccupied with the problems of the office or factory that no real relationship with him is possible. In each of these instances the father is 'absent'. It is the emotional atmosphere which is important. The *way* father responds to the infant is the essential feature of his physical presence—though obviously if he is not there he cannot respond at all.

Father's absence, whether actual or emotional, temporary or complete, means that one corner of the mother-father-infant triangle is missing. Inevitably, therefore, while father is absent the child's relationships, his demands, his needs are directed solely towards the mother and must be exclusively fulfilled by her. Moreover a young child has virtually no capacity for memory or for seeing ahead: and he cannot recollect his absent father in the way his mother can. She has many associations to keep her husband alive in her memory, and in her affection. Even though she may miss him greatly, the bond with him can remain intact. But for the child it is almost literally a question of 'out of sight; out of mind'. His relationship with mother must inevitably become more possessive, demanding and strong. In such circumstances it is difficult for the child to learn to 'share' his mother with anyone else or accept the giving as well as the taking of a more mature relationship. It will be more than usually difficult for his mother to help him to do so. Indeed, to some extent her own feeling of loss from her husband's absence will tempt her to make her own bond with her child even more possessive than it would otherwise be. For she too has lost a corner of the family triangle.

The longer or more complete is father's absence, the harder it will be for the young child (whether boy or girl) to build up a model of the masculine pattern and role.

Even if father's absence is temporary, his return may produce new complications; complications which may come as a complete surprise to those concerned.

While he was away, both husband and wife may well have built up an idealized picture of what home life used to be like and what it will be like after his return. Part of this imagined picture may well comprise a happy reunited family having the fun together that they have missed.

But when the father does return he finds he is something of an intruder. His wife may welcome him; but because of the strong exclusive mutual bond that has grown between her and their child, many a returning father has heard his child ask how soon he will be going away again, so that mother and child can be together again.

It is perfectly understandable that the child should respond in this way, but for the other two members of the triangle the problem is very real. The returning husband and father feels a stranger in his home, whilst wondering why he is not automatically accepted back as father. He may accuse his wife of 'spoiling' the child whereas what he is really expressing is his resentment at the close bond between them that seems to have as yet no place for him.

His wife, too, may be caught off-guard by the very nature of her own mixed feelings. Because she is glad to have her husband home it may be all the more difficult for her to recognize that his presence is a disruption of her exclusive relationship with the child. She may express this by telling her husband that he does not know how to 'manage' the child, or is too harsh with him, when what she is really feeling is 'Leave him to me!'

Such a returning father, dismayed by the reception he is actually getting, in contrast to the idealized version he had been expecting, may try to force his way into the family pattern and by so doing only intensify the feeling that he is an intruder. Such efforts may produce the reverse effects to those he wanted; and serve to make the bond between mother and child even closer and more exclusive.

Or the father may give up his attempt and go to the opposite extremes of feeling (and perhaps even saying) 'Oh, all right then, if you don't want me then I don't need you'. He may lose interest in the family and adopt a 'don't care' attitude that masks his bitter feeling of rejection. Sometimes such fathers actually leave home, but more often they continue to live there almost as an unimplicated lodger, speaking to their wives about 'Your child' if they mention him at all. Inevitably a vicious circle builds up and intensifies the difficulty instead of alleviating it; mother and child become closer still, feeling that father is against them. All this must intensify the child's difficulty in learning to share his basic relationship and in learning at first-hand a pattern of masculinity that is so important for his development. He cannot achieve this if his father is so isolated from any feeling-relationship for him that they are virtually strangers. We cannot pattern ourselves adequately on someone with whom we have no real relationship.

The difficulty or ease with which a family can settle down and re-establish the triangle of family living will depend to a considerable degree on the early experiences of the two adults. If the father or mother had special difficulty in being (or feeling) the 'unwanted one' of their own primary relationships or over later contacts they will find it correspondingly difficult to cope with a similar challenge at this stage.

A rather similar situation can arise when a stepfather comes into a family. If his new wife has a young child there may be considerable difficulties. The bond between mother and child may be even more intense, following her bereavement, than in the illustration which we described above. The child may have seen the stepfather, or even know him quite well. But that is not the same as having to share mother with him day by day. And as with a returning father, so the stepfather may feel the child is antagonistic to him; and that the child, and therefore the mother, do not really want him. He, too, may try to force the pace or buy or bribe his way into the affections of the child. Or, if the situation is too difficult for him, he may give up the struggle and withdraw from any real attempt at relationship with the child.

If we consider the paternal role as important, then we must describe the relationship with the mother during those early years of the infant's life as vital and completely essential. There are some obvious biological (as well as emotional) reasons why the mother is the most important figure at this stage. She has carried the child within her own body during pregnancy, and gone through the trials of labour to bring him into the world. She is normally the person most concerned with his care and feeding; and as such she had the most, the closest and the earliest physical contact with him. We know from studies of animal behaviour how soon (and surely) the new-born animal can recognize its mother; and how vital this recognition may be to his survival. There is evidence to show that the human infant can identify his own mother from a very early age; and much to suggest that he does this through his more primitive senses, and especially through physical contact.

The work of Bowlby and his associates, however, has shown that there is a deeper significance to this relationship; and that what we call 'mothering' is vital to the young child's development and progress in every sphere. Although Bowlby's views have been strongly criticized in some quarters, and considerably 'oversold' by some of his too enthusiastic supporters, it would be generally agreed that his concepts of the significance of mother-infant relationships has been one of the major contributions in the field of mental health. It would be outside the scope of a book of this type to study this controversy in detail. The interested reader will find a balanced and readable multi-disciplinary assessment of present day views of this topic in World Health Organization Public Health Papers No. 14— 'Deprivation of Maternal Care: A Re-assessment of its Effects', 1962.

Briefly, however, the only real controversy is over the permanence and inevitability of damage from such deprivation; and over the exact nature of 'mothering'.

As a general indication of the pattern of this problem as it appears in clinical practice we have felt that it would be useful to reproduce here from a previous publication[1] an actual example from personal experience.

[1] National Marriage Guidance Council Training Booklet No. 7—
Dr T. A. Ratcliffe

'After the war there were very large numbers of refugee children in Europe who literally knew nothing at all about their parents. A certain agency (a very good one, incidentally) set up two small children's residential nurseries in Germany for such children under three years of age. Both nurseries were very well run, with high standards of medical and nursing care, of building, diet and staffing ratio. There were about twenty children in each, and to all intents and purposes the two nurseries were identical. The children were not in any way selected—all were refugee children who had no parents. These nurseries were very well supervised; and it was found rather mysteriously that entirely different results were being obtained between the two of them. In one of them the children were unmistakeably progressing better than in the other, in terms of physical development, freedom from illness, absence of behaviour problems, in learning to talk and walk and so on. This led, not unnaturally, to a close study of the diet scale and hygienic conditions of the two nurseries by the responsible paediatric experts. But no difference could be observed. Finally it was decided to change over the two matrons. Very soon the trends were reversed.

'Both matrons, however, were highly qualified, highly competent people and in every material way both were looking after the children and running the nursery with admirable efficiency. But they were nevertheless very different kinds of people. One of them was an extremely efficient but emotionally very hard, 'tough' woman; the other a very warm, motherly, affectionate person. We will not insult the reader by suggesting which was achieving the better results!'

This example vividly illustrates the important distinction between affective mothering and efficient material caring. Mothering, in this sense, includes loving a child and letting him know he is loved by experiencing it. It seems certain that the infant senses this love through physical contact, and that factors such as body warmth, smell and the touch of mother's handling play an important part. So probably does the comfort of being fed and the process of sucking. But one is tempted to postulate also that the child may be able to 'sense' in some specific primitive way the 'atmosphere' created by his mother's love.

But the example quoted illustrates another important aspect of this problem, namely that deprivation of mother-love produces its damage over the whole wide area of infantile development, physical as well as emotional and social and in the learning of individual skills.

Finally, since the children in our example had already lost their own mothers before the story begins, it illustrates also the role of a 'substitute mother'. We will be returning to this aspect later in this chapter.

One place in which a careful observational study can be made of the infant's reaction to deprivation is in hospital, particularly if the child has been admitted for some relatively minor procedure and is not seriously ill. Illness could produce complicating factors.

A little girl of four was admitted to hospital unconscious with an illness that was not at first diagnosable. For perfectly proper medical reasons, she was isolated. Her mother was allowed to visit her only twice a week. Although she was not long in hospital, it took nearly a year for her to settle down at home with her brothers and sisters and parents and get back to the stage she had reached before her illness. And then quite suddenly she began to regress, became disturbed and anxious and would not leave mother's side. Her mother realized that there was probably a link between the appearance of Christmas decorations and this change, since her illness had occurred the previous Christmas. She therefore explained to her daughter that if she should ever have another illness and have to go to hospital, mother would go with her. This reassurance, which she was old enough and trusting enough to accept, enabled her to get over her set-back. Fourteen years later she suffered actutely from 'home-sickness' at the start of her residential training—in hospital. Her mother visited her and she gradually settled down.

When a very young child is first admitted to hospital without mother, he passes through three successive stages of reaction. His first and immediate reaction is one of panic and bewilderment. His one sure source of confidence, his mother, has suddenly vanished. He is surrounded by strange people in strange and rather frightening surroundings. The shock of separation from mother will be all the greater if he has been tricked into believing that mother will be with him again in a few minutes. With good and understanding handling this panic may subside quite soon. Although basically he remains anxious and apprehensive and may return to bed wetting or thumb sucking, sleep badly or go off his food, he will, in fact, become quiet and rather withdrawn. To the busy ward staff he may seem to have 'settled down'. Attempts to contact him may meet with considerable resistance. This resistance may even occur when the mother visits, just as the acute apprehension may build up again when her visit ends; and quickly subside into the rather withdrawn phase.

This second stage of reaction which we have described may continue unchanged for some weeks. The importance of this stage is its reversibility. Provided there is some contact with the mother and provided that the total period of separation is not too long (the actual crucial period is probably individual to each child, but in general terms the maximum 'safe' separation would seem to be about three weeks) it is doubtful if any *permanent* damage is done to the infant.

When he returns home after such a relatively short separation, the infant may well react as did the four-year old described above. But this is essentially a temporary, and very understandable, phase of insecurity.

If the separation is prolonged, however, a third, and permanently damaged, stage of deprivation will develop.

The child becomes more withdrawn and even apathetic. It is as though he has finally despaired since the essential security of his life has been lost; and neither panic nor anxiety can be tolerated longer. He now shows no feelings of any kind. He has isolated himself from a world with which he has no feeling-relationship. He is now amenable, quiet, no trouble to anyone

47

and it is small wonder that he is sometimes described as having 'settled down', 'quite happy—he's no trouble at all'. It is as though something dies within him, the ability to trust anyone enough to form a relationship with them. He is denying his basic need to make relationships with others. It has become difficult or even impossible to make any kind of affectionate or accepting relationship with him and he will go through life isolated from its warmth, with no stake in the well-being of others and allowing them no stake in his.

This is the picture of severe deprivation. This is what a client meant (although he did not then see its meaning and thought of it only as a 'slip of the tongue') when he said in a case-work interview: 'When my mother was three, I died.' But it must be emphasized again that there are varying degrees and depths of reaction. The severity will vary with the length and age of initial separation and with the quality of mothering which the child enjoyed before and after that primary loss. There is also clinical evidence which strongly suggests a constitutional variation as between individual children in their vulnerability to the loss of maternal love.

Admission to hospital is not, of course, the only way in which separation of mother and infant can arise. But it is the area in which a great deal can be done most easily to minimize the risk of subsequent damage, by regular frequent visiting, by the avoidance of unnecessary hospitalization for very young children, by training hospital staffs towards a greater understanding of the problem: and, in suitable instances, by taking mother and young child into hospital together.

But in our present stage of civilization and knowledge there is much less that we can do to prevent the very serious loss of maternal care which arises from the death, desertion, divorce or prolonged illness of the mother.

If relatively little can be done to prevent such situations, it is clearly of vital importance to consider how these possibly dangerous consequences to the infant can be minimized or relieved. Fortunately, although the child's own mother is the natural and usual source of maternal love, adequate mothering can be carried through quite adequately when necessary by a substitute-mother, provided, that is, that the chosen substitute fulfils certain essential requirements. First she must be able to be genuinely 'motherly' towards this particular child. What has been called 'synthetic affection' will not provide for the infant's needs. Primarily, of course, this capacity to be motherly depends on the personality and life-experiences of the individual concerned; but some people may well feel antipathy to a particular type of child, or be more able spontaneously to have feelings for a girl than a boy, or for a handicapped child and so on. It must never be forgotten that this is a two-way relationship and that both infant and substitute-mother must be able to 'take to' each other in every emotional sense.

But the substitute-mother must be one person, and not a whole series of people. The relationship is a person-to-person one and the small child has little or no capacity to accept changes in his substitute parent. But it is not only at the beginnings of such a substitute relationship that the mother-figure must remain constant and the same person. The child whose primary parental relations have 'let him down' must remain very vulnerable to any future experience of (or even risk of) rejection, as the following illustration (from the previously quoted publication by the author) will show.

'Her mother looked after her for the first two years or so but was not in the least interested in her and decided to have her adopted. She was adopted by a woman who wanted her for purely self-centred reasons, because it was the accepted thing to have a child in her particular social group. When the child was about nine the adoptive mother lost interest in her and took her to court as being beyond her control. She was then taken into the care of the local authority and since then she has moved around from one foster home to another. In each she could not settle but she became (administratively) a great nuisance. By the time she came to us, at eleven or twelve, she was almost unable to make any contacts. She would talk to people, and meet them, but without any kind of feeling for them. After a great deal of slow and laborious and careful work we began to

49

build some sort of bridge with this girl and establish some sort of emotional contact with her. Then, quite suddenly, for purely administrative reasons, she was moved to another children's home. The whole structure of her developing relationship collapsed and it is unlikely now that it will ever be possible to rebuild it. You may say that she was not really rejected on these later occasions; that she was moved for perfectly adequate administrative reasons. But to her, it was a rejection and it came at a critical point, just when she was beginning to make her first real emotional relationships.'

However, even when these criteria for suitable substitute-mothering are suitably provided, the building up of an adequate relationship with the child is no simple or automatic process. Indeed, when the effects of deprivation are really severe, only long-term skilled psychotherapy may be successful. Although it is understandable, it is in many ways unfortunate that so often the ordinary average foster-mother is assumed to be capable of this difficult task without a great deal more help and support than she often receives. It is no easy task to continue to 'give' to the deprived child for many months when, by reason of his disability, the child is unable to give any response in return. Equally, the child who has suffered earlier deprivations will need to be mothered at that level of infantile development which he has missed. It is not easy for the ordinary foster-mother in an ordinary family and home to handle a child of six who is at the emotional and social level of a two-year old.

It is no contradiction of our basic principles, therefore, to say that there will be some deprived children who can be helped more in the less emotionally demanding setting of a good children's home rather than in a foster situation. And it must not be forgotten that the failure of a foster-placement, and the consequent re-rejection of the child, must be gravely damaging.

CHAPTER IV

The Basic Conflict

As we saw in a previous chapter, every child from earliest infancy is faced by an inevitable conflict. This is the conflict between what he wants to do and what he is able or allowed to do. Or it may be between what he wants to have and what he is permitted to have.

On the one hand are his instinctual drives, on the other limitations set by his own capability and the adult demands or prohibitions to which he must conform. This conflict, in various forms, is basic to the whole of his life. Indeed, one of the best criteria of adult maturity is the measure of success a person has achieved in balancing his instinctual drives against the demands of society, and in redirecting these primitive drives into socially constructive channels.

In earliest infancy this balance and redirection come about by the physical control of the mother and father who handle him. Even if inadequately, the infant tries to co-operate with, and to please, the parent and so to win approval. At first this occurs only when the parent is physically present although quite quickly the parent can operate by 'remote control'. Gradually this external control is replaced by internal self-control. The child begins to develop a set of personal and internal standards, the rudiments of his own 'conscience'.

This process of development and change may be considered in various ways and be explained in terms of different psychological theories. It is our aim here to illustrate the common ground between these various approaches.

Let us first consider a simple and primitive situation. A man walking along a jungle path comes face to face with a lion. He is immediately confronted with two main alternatives, to stand firm in the face of imminent danger or to run away. The instinctual response to this situation is to feel afraid and run for safety. Nevertheless and in spite of this reaction, he may stand fast and attack the lion as best he can. There is also a third possibility, that he will dither between these alternatives and be unable to decide which to take. What main factors may influence his decision?

The more obvious and overt factors arise from his previous experience. How has he dealt with similar situations before? What skills has he learnt which might help in tackling a lion single-handed? More subtly (but at a conscious, thought-out level) how does he rate his chances of success? Besides these factors and allied to them, will be his assessment of how dangerous is this particular lion, in this particular situation. This assessment also will be based on his past experience.

Suppose this situation is a little more complicated and the sudden chance encounter is watched by a companion from a distance, who is too far away to help. What will this companion think of him if he runs away or on the contrary if he stands firm and kills the lion? These factors also will influence him. There is also his feeling of duty to his companion, who may be endangered if he runs away and escapes.

Further, there will be the opinion of his fellow villagers, whether he returns having killed the lion or arrives terrified, having run away from it. Will he exceed their expectations of him or will he fail to live up to the tradition of his tribe or his family?

And then, what does he expect of himself? Will he feel justified in his own eyes in running away or will he feel ashamed even if no one knows about the incident?

There may also be internal factors (arising from his own phantasy and imagination) that influence his decision. The former factors arose out of the reality of his present predicament and his previous experience. These latter factors do not arise from reality. He may have a primitive and unreasonably powerful fear of lions based not on actual experience but (say) on religious or superstitious traditions within his tribe. Or, on the contrary, he may have an equally unreal phantasy picture of himself as a fearless and successful hero and lion-killer, like Tartarin of Tarascon. These 'non-reality' factors may influence his decision even more powerfully than the reality factors, even though they too are fully conscious.

This example illustrates something of the complexity of the way we react to situations that threaten or confront us. Most of us are inclined to under-rate the importance of phantasy and to dismiss it as something we have outgrown; or at most as a mere relic of immaturity or infancy. It is certainly true that our phantasy life was at its most vivid and powerful during early childhood. Indeed, very young children are often unable to distinguish between reality and phantasy. They live a large part of their time in a rich phantasy world of their own creation. In the course of play-therapy for example one can sometimes see a child 'solve' the real problems of his life by the way he learns to handle similar situations in his phantasy world.

As we grow up we learn to distinguish more clearly between the phantasy world and the world of reality. But even the mature adult has not moved finally out of his own private phantasy world. For example, suppose through our own incompetence or lack of confidence (which we may not admit openly) we have lost an argument with the boss. Most of us will spend the bus journey home re-creating in imagination an interview in which we are victorious. Another measure of our maturity lies in the degree to which we are able to recognize the unpleasant fact that this day-dream in no way influences what actually took place. Though it may influence our attitude the next time, it does not affect the reality of our humiliating defeat.

The concept of the unconscious adds a further step to and beyond our understanding of the role that phantasy takes in our lives as in much else in human behaviour. The commonly-held belief that most human decisions and actions are the product of rational and deliberate thought, is demonstrably false.

The direct evidence of our senses only has meaning for us when it has been interpreted through the central co-ordinating mechanism of the brain. But it is not always interpreted correctly or accurately. There is ample evidence from experimental psychology to confirm this and we can also find examples from everyday life. A husband who does not notice the new hat his wife is wearing has misinterpreted the evidence of his own eyes. His mind visualizes her as he expected her to look rather than correctly interpreting the visual evidence of how she does look. Similarly, one may misread the name of a character in a book as 'Geoffrey' when what is actually written and actually 'seen' by our eyes is 'Godfrey'. And then, in all probability, we shall continue so to misread it throughout.

We are not aware of these errors of perception until they have been pointed out to us. In that sense, they can be ascribed to unconscious activity. Certain errors of this type can be explained in terms of brain functioning but others cannot be adequately explained except in terms of unconscious motivation.

When we come into contact with a new person or a new situation (like the man facing the lion) we assess the position; but our assessment is coloured by our past experience and by pre-judgements that have arisen from it. This colouring is not only immediate and temporary but may continue and be deeply seated. Yet such 'errors' and a great deal of the experience that gives rise to them lie outside the area of our conscious thinking.

When we have to confront (say) a policeman or a headmaster, the way we see him will be coloured in part by our past experience of authority figures, including the experience of our own child-father relationship. Similar factors affect the choice of those we like or dislike. These also are partly coloured by such unconscious factors. The way we behave and react will be similarly affected.

One can easily over-estimate, or under-estimate, the significance of unconscious feelings and motivations. A social worker interviewing an unresponsive client may interpret the lack of response in terms of possible unconscious factors without considering that it may arise directly from the uncomfortable setting of the interview or from clearcut and fully conscious problems that the client may have on his mind at that moment. In very general terms, we can say that the unconscious factors frequently influence what we *feel* and what we *think* but that most of the *actions* we perform are under conscious control.

The human mind can be considered as functioning on three 'levels', though these do not correspond to three anatomical divisions of the brain.

At the conscious level are those thoughts, ideas and feelings of which we are aware at the time. The content of this level is constantly changing and there is a continual interchange between this level and the next, the pre-conscious level. This latter, in everyday terms, is the memory. Thoughts and ideas and feelings constantly pass into memory, others constantly emerge from it into consciousness. It is generally relatively easy to make these exchanges between the conscious and pre-conscious levels of functioning though the interchange may be hampered on occasion by anxiety, fatigue or faulty concentration or ill health.

The third level of functioning is unconscious. At this level lie all those experiences and the emotional responses originally linked to them, together with ideas and thoughts dating back to our earliest years. We are not normally aware of this deeply stored material nor even of its existence. We cannot recall material from it, or put material into it, at will. We cannot choose what material is to be hidden in this way or what brought to the conscious level. Nevertheless, there is strong evidence to show that our conscious activity is affected by this deeper material, usually indirectly.

A simple analogy will illustrate these points. In any home there are a great many items in immediate use, books, knives, forks, radio, furniture and so on. These correspond to the contents of the conscious layer of the mind. There are also many items put away in cupboards and drawers and on shelves, ready for use and quickly obtainable when needed. This 'ready-for-use' storage compares with the pre-conscious level of the mind. Finally, most houses have some store-room or attic where items that, as we say, 'might come in handy some day' have been relegated haphazard. We cannot remember all that is there and we may have a vague, distorted recollection about some of them. This represents in our analogy the unconscious level.

We can carry this analogy a stage further. If we go into this store room, for something we vaguely remember, and start looking for it we shall not be able to follow any ordered way of searching. As we explore we come across many articles which we had forgotten. Some of these may arouse memories and associations and even emotions arising from the original incident with which the object was connected. And even if we do find what we are looking for, it may be different from how we remembered it.

At the unconscious level of our mind lie those primitive and powerful instinctive wishes and emotions which were the driving force of our infantile activity and which still remain the most potent source of psychic energy.

From this analogy we can visualize the basic conflict between the buried, hidden and forgotten unconscious forces within us and the controls put upon them from the environment, or which the environment has forced us to make for ourselves. In our analogy, the dusty and forgotten articles in the store room lay quietly there out of mind. But (and here our analogy does not quite hold) the contents of the unconscious level of the mind do not always lie quiet but are more like creatures straining to get out, and whether we know it or not, we may have difficulty in keeping them there or explaining their presence to ourselves or to other people.

We can imagine this conflict in the form of a diagram as three circles with the same centre. Right outside the whole lies the outside world, the environment. In the outer ring is the Ego—our personality or ourselves as we appear to the world. Then comes a band that comprises the Super-ego, whose function it is to defend the ego and the outside world against the contents of the inmost circle. This last is what is known in psychoanalytic terms as the Id. Here lie the unconscious, primitive, instinctive drives.

In chapter V we shall describe how the super-ego develops and functions.

CHAPTER V

Mental Mechanisms

It may often seem relatively easy to understand the motivations and behaviour of the very young child; and, indeed, it quite often *is* a simple matter. But, as the child grows up, it is obvious that his behaviour and reactions, and the motivations behind them, become increasingly sophisticated, complex and difficult to understand.

It is not surprising, therefore, that many theories have been advanced to explain such motivations and the mechanisms by which they work. Such theories began with the idea of demoniac possession and of the influence of the various bodily 'humours'; and have moved through various philosophical approaches to the beginnings of psychological theory in the early part of this century. Since then fresh, stimulating and highly significant theories have been developed, elaborated, and (at least to some degree) validated by clinical experience. From the social psychology of McDougall and through the vital new concepts of Freud, Jung and their followers to the recent work of Eysenck, each approach has contributed something—and often a great deal—of value to the study of human behaviour. Unfortunately, each theoretical approach has tended to be so enthusiastically, and sometimes blindly, received by its followers that each basic concept is 'oversold' as the one and only possible theory.

It would be beyond the scope of this book either to describe all the varied theoretical concepts,[1] or argue out in detail their relative merits or truths. And it is not possible to provide a description of mental mechanisms, however selective this may

---

[1] Readers who wish for further details will find a clear, if brief, account of virtually all the various schools of thought in this field in Dr Nicolle's *Psychopathology*. Bailliere, Tindall and Cox.

be, that will not provoke strong disagreement from the more ardent followers of one or other of the various schools of psychopathology.

It would be equally impracticable to cover the whole field of mental mechanisms in any detail in one short chapter. We shall endeavour, therefore, to describe some of the more important bases of human behaviour within a theoretical framework that will be reasonably acceptable to the majority. We shall deal straight-forwardly and as simply as possible with those aspects of theory which have the most obvious practical implications for those whose task it is to help others with their problems.

In the previous chapter we considered the basic, and in our view vital, concept of the unconscious and conscious levels of mental functioning; and we gave some instances of the relative significance of conscious and unconscious factors in human behaviour. But since this balance is fundamental to any understanding of mental mechanisms it must be explored further here.

It has been said that the motivation of all human behaviour stems from the unconscious. In part this is certainly true, since clearly much of what we do or feel or think is affected by long-forgotten experiences and by basic instinctual drives. Nor, obviously, do we always make our decisions on a conscious, or even on an entirely rational, basis.

Even allowing for this aspect, however, it is essential not to minimize the importance of immediate reality situations with which we are confronted day by day; and of our consciously made decisions. It is probably truer to say that unconscious material colours our feelings and decisions than that such material actually governs them.

We must consider another aspect of human motivation, however; and one which it is difficult to allot either to a wholly conscious or a wholly unconscious level.

The complex mechanics involved in walking have originally to be specfically learnt; but once we have learnt this technique we can walk without thinking about it. Even when some modification of our walking technique becomes necessary, due perhaps to a painful ankle, this is equally achieved without conscious thought on our part.

Although the example chosen here is virtually an entirely 'mechanical' process, a somewhat similar process can be envisaged in the wider field of behaviour and motivation. There seems no doubt that a long and gradual conditioning process whereby we specifically learn certain responses to certain situations can eventually convert this into a habit of response. Such habit patterns may be modified by new experience, but their strength stems from the degree to which these habit responses perpetuate, and are built up from, conventional cultural standards. Conditioning, and for that matter de-conditioning, are closely linked also to our desire to seek approval and comfort; and to avoid their opposites.

Consequently as we grow up we gradually replace, at least partly, our dependence on external standards and controls by our own internal and personal standards. All these varying conscious, unconscious and conditioning factors influence the development, strength and form of that personal controlling mechanism which we have called the super-ego. We still seek the approval and avoid disapproval especially from those with whom we have close relationships; but we also aim to avoid that disapproval of our super-ego, which we call guilt.

In the previous chapter we visualized largely in conscious terms the basic conflict between what I wish to do and what I can or ought to do. We need now to see this in more sophisticated terms as a parallel conflict between our instinctive drives and our super-ego. Or, in other words, the attempt of the id to force its way past our super-ego in the latter's attempted balance with our external environment. Clearly there can be conflicts which are conducted wholly consciously, when we will be aware both of the origins of the conflict and our decision —which is also made consciously. At the other extreme there may well be a conflict which is deeply unconscious and of whose existence we become aware only when its result impacts onto our conscious thinking or into our actual actions. For the most part, however, such conflicts, although influenced by unconscious, and conditioned, factors will be resolved by conscious processes.

The term conflict used in this context is possibly an unfortunate one since it implies an absolute victory of one side at the total expense and surrender of the other. Such absolute victories do sometimes occur. If (to use everyday terms) the temptation to do something is very strong and our in-built resistance to that particular temptation is weak, then we may give way to it completely and with virtually no subsequent feelings of guilt. If, at the other extreme, our super-ego is excessively harsh and powerful we may be able to 'block off' completely (if only probably for a limited time) strong instinctual drives and desires. But, for the most part, we should visualize the controlling mechanism not as an absolute block, but as a tap which can be turned on, partly or wholly, as well as off; and as a selective mechanism which can redirect and re-channel such drives into more socially—, and personally-acceptable forms. Thus the solution of most conflicts is reached through a compromise decision which tries to combine the best features of the instinctual drives and of the standards desired by the controlling mechanism.

The purpose of quite a number of mental mechanisms is to facilitate this type of compromise solution of conflicts. We have already described sublimation in general terms as the conversion of basic drives and desires into forms which are socially more acceptable; or into a form which will satisfy the standards which our super-ego demands. This is an important and much used process. Through it, potentially (and sometimes actually) destructive reactions such as jealousy, anger or aggression can be converted into constructive forces which power much of human activity. Of course we can, and do, make such compromises and decisions, consciously and deliberately; but strictly speaking, sublimations refer essentially to modifications made under super-ego control. Since, as we have seen, the super-ego builds up its standards from past (and usually forgotten) experiences, this means that sublimation is essentially unconsciously motivated. Consequently there can be considerable apparent illogicality in such a sublimated action. Sometimes what is acceptable to our super-ego may not be socially accept-able in our environment; and vice-versa. (It is an interesting social corollary to this illogicality that the 'liberal thinker' who claims that, as sex is a natural instinct it should have no taboos or controls will equally claim that aggression—an equally natural instinctual drive—should be given no outlets of any sort at all.)

Projection is another mechanism by which we can side-step a conflict situation. For there we project our feelings or desires onto some object or person. There are two principal ways in which this can be done. In the one most commonly described, we condemn particularly those faults in others in which we ourselves basically like to indulge, but which our super-ego strictly prohibits. But we can also project our feelings more openly and directly than this.

If, for example, a husband and wife quarrel, it may happen that the husband rushes off to his office still smouldering with anger which, for a variety of reasons, he could not bring out openly to his wife. Once at the office he may project this anger on to his secretary over some minor fault; an anger-response quite out of proportion to the incident. His secretary may not feel able to answer back adequately; she in turn may need to take it out of the office boy. He, having no one lower in the social scale, may kick the office cat. It is clear in this example that each in turn has projected on their anger; and that the office cat is really receiving the initial anger of the husband towards his wife. Although anger is possibly the emotion most commonly involved in this mechanism, we can project any other feeling.

This process is important both in the normal forms in which we all use it, and in its excessive and abnormal forms. But it is one of special significance to the social worker and to the therapist. For he may often be the 'office cat' who receives the projected hostility, suspicion or dependancy which the client is unable or unwilling to direct towards the person for whom it is really intended.

A somewhat similar mechanism is our use of identification. If we read a book, or watch a play or a film, we often identify ourselves with one of the characters. By this quite normal process we may greatly increase our enjoyment; but through it we can indulge (if only in phantasy) in activities and feelings which we could not permit ourselves in real life. As with every mental mechanism, the degree to which identification is used can vary between normal limits to the point when we confuse phantasy with reality. Equally we may use this process to release either conscious or unconsciously motivated desires.

The use of symbolic concepts that express attitudes and feelings too complex to define in detail, is quite common. If one talks of loyalty to the Crown, or to the national flag, one is clearly using such objects as the symbol for an elaborate and possibly very mixed set of feelings. But we also use symbols to 'cover up' for ideas and desires which would be unacceptable to our super-ego or to the external standards and conventions of our environment. We use symbols also in our dreams and in our phantasy thinking for very much the same reasons. If a symbol is to be successful in this context it must be an adequate 'cover' but also be sufficiently representative of the basic drive to allow the adequate release of that drive. The source of these symbols is our unconscious mind; and our choice of a particular symbol is normally outside our conscious control. Many of our symbols stem from forgotten past experience; and since we all have much general past experience in common, it is not surprising that certain symbols are in common use to represent specific underlying concepts. Nevertheless, it would be unwise to assume that any given symbol *must* have the same meaning for everyone on all occasions. A reasonable analogy would be the way in which various articles can be used in the old-fashioned game of Dumb-Crambo. In this game we use whatever object is to be found amongst the lumber of the household to represent what we need for our dramatic performance. Thus, in Act 1, a golf club may be the symbol for a king's sceptre, in Act 2 it may represent an oar—and in Act 3 it might even portray a golf club. Similarly the symbolic mechanisms need to be interpreted not rigidly, but within the context of the individual's past experience and emotional needs.

Despite the use of such mechanisms, a situation may arise

when the conflict cannot be resolved. If the two opposing forces of basic desire and control are so evenly balanced that neither can win (either fully or in part) a feeling of uncertainty arises—a feeling of anxiety. Such a state of anxiety may arise when we cannot decide on a consciously decided choice between two alternatives of action. If, for example, we cannot decide whether to accept a particular job or decline it, we feel unsure, and therefore anxious. Equally, however, the unresolved conflict may be at an unconscious level. In that case there is the same consequent anxiety, although now one feels anxious without knowing what one is anxious about.

A feeling of anxiety is uncomfortable, particularly if we do not know its cause. After all, in such circumstances, we cannot even begin to tackle our problem since we do not know its real nature, or limits. The relief of this intolerable situation is provided by one of these following mental mechanisms.

If we are anxious, then certain inevitable physical responses occur. We shall be aware of these symptoms and our anxiety can easily be transposed from the original and unconscious conflict to the bodily symptoms themselves. Or, by an alternative but similar mechanism, the anxiety may be transposed from the basic conflict onto some specific (and often symbolic) object or situation. Then we have a phobic anxiety about (say) the dark, or snakes or high places. (In ordinary speech we tend to describe such phobias as 'fear' of the object: but technically they represent anxiety rather than fear.)

We do not rid ourselves of anxiety by either of these mechanisms; but at least we have now a peg on which to hang it. We no longer have that intolerable sense of uncertainty without apparent cause. At least we can now be anxious about our particular bodily symptoms or about our specific phobia. Although our action may not prove to be constructive in any long-term sense, we can at least attempt to combat the symptom; or evade the phobic situation. In practice, of course, the opposite may occur. For, if we are now anxious about the symptom or the phobia this may increase our anxiety—and therefore increase these transposed symptoms.

A further, and rather more dramatic, mechanism with the

same basic purpose, is the hysterical response. Although the motivation and mechanics of this process occur at an unconscious level, it is usually relatively easy to link the reactions to the original reality situation which produced the conflict. Consequently an hysterical response can often be seen as a convenient escape from an intolerable situation. We may confuse such a response with overt malingering; and almost always there is some conscious dramatization super-imposed upon the hysterical symptom. It is best, therefore, to illustrate this mechanism by one of the more dramatic examples.

If a soldier in war-time knows he is to go into battle on the next day he will be faced with a conflict situation—a conflict between the fear-driven desire to escape from this danger and his guilt-driven need to face up to the situation. In simpler terms, the conflict is between desertion from the battlefield or going into action with all its obvious dangers.

Obviously such a conflict may be resolved at a conscious level of decision; but more usually the solution occurs unconsciously, so that our decision to run away or face up to danger appears in our consciousness with little or no preliminary reasoning. In most instances, too, the decision is clear-cut and we take one or other of the possible actions. Suppose, however, that the conflict is so evenly balanced that neither solution can 'win'. A state of uncertainty, of anxiety, will result.

If this anxiety can be converted within the framework of an hysterical reaction and at an unconscious level, it will appear as a disabling symptom. In the illustration which we have given above, the soldier may convert his anxiety to (say) an hysterical blindness or paralysis or to some other symptom. If this occurs, an immediate (if not a long term) solution to the conflict has been found. For, now, the soldier can be removed from the battlefield as an honourable casualty. He need neither run away nor face up to the danger.

The more we consider this solution, however, the less satisfactory it becomes, for the soldier has exchanged his conflict for a disabling symptom. Nor can that symptom be relieved, or given up, until the basic and original conflict has been satisfactorily worked out.

Such an hysterical response as has been so far described would be pathological; but milder and normal reactions of this type are used by all of us from time to time. If we have made a dental appointment which we feel we should keep, we may equally be tempted not to face up to it. In such circumstances we may forget the appointment. This, in a minor and quite normal way, is an hysterical loss of memory; and it is equally an unsatisfactory solution to the original problem.

This same broad spread between severe or pathological emotional disturbance and normal response applies to the whole wide spectrum of mental mechanisms and emotional reactions. Anxiety can be used as an example of this.

Anxiety, like anger or jealousy or guilt or other similar reactions, are normal and necessary defence mechanisms; a mechanism which protects us from danger, or from going too far. Anxiety, therefore, can be, and often is, normal. But anxiety can also be severely disabling and abnormal. The boundaries between these two levels are not always easy to define. There are, however, two worthwhile criteria which can be used in this differentiation.

In general terms we can say that anxiety has passed beyond the point of normality if it is so severe as to be disabling and interferes with our capacity to function adequately. To take a simple example, it is reasonable and normal to feel anxiety before an examination; but if that anxiety is so severe or so disabling that it prevents us from performing up to our capacity in the examination itself, then it has clearly become a disability rather than a normal defence mechanism.

The second criterion for this differentiation is the degree to which the severity of the anxiety is justified by its apparent, or actual, cause. But this can be a much more complex and difficult judgment to make. For we must always consider whether the anxiety is reasonable for this particular individual in his particular circumstances at that particular time.

It is reasonable and normal that a mother will feel anxious when her child makes his first journeys to and from school on his own. On the basis of our first criterion, such anxiety would become pathological if it was so severe that it prevented

65

her from letting her child take this necessary risk at a reasonable age and stage of development. If, however, the journey to school involved crossing busy main roads, or if a neighbour's child had recently been sexually assaulted on such a journey, or the mother had herself been involved in a serious traffic accident, then a greater degree of anxiety could be accepted as still normal.

The illustrations given above all represent 'reactive anxiety', where there is an overt and conscious trigger for the anxiety. As we have seen, anxiety may also stem from unconscious conflict; and may then have no obvious trigger. It is tempting to equate reactive anxiety with normal anxiety; and to consider deep anxiety as pathological. This is certainly not an absolute truth. Nevertheless, when we have an anxiety pattern which is both reactive and stemming from unconscious conflict (and this is a not unusual combination) the additional deep anxiety will clearly tend to cross those boundaries between normal and pathological anxiety which we have defined here.

CHAPTER VI

Learning and Intelligence

Without the ability to learn we could not survive, either as individuals or collectively. Certainly learning (in one sense of the word) plays an essential part in the development of our personality.

Once a child can walk and talk and dress himself and generally fit in with the family routine and once he starts school, it is tempting to think that his learning will be mainly confined to school work. We may say that a part of this process will consist of learning how to behave, learning necessary standards and learning how to stick up for himself or take defeat or keep his temper, and so on. But we tend, perhaps, to feel that the essential learning is the subjects he will be taught.

Some children learn quickly and easily and we speak of them as clever. Yet we use this word to convey different shades of meaning. Sometimes it means 'smart' in a rather questionable sense, conveying 'clever-clever' or 'too clever by half' or even shady, as people say with a knowing look that someone had 'a clever lawyer' when what they mean is that in strict honesty or justice things would have gone differently. Sometimes we use the word 'intelligent' as a more praiseworthy version of clever and sometimes 'clever' is used to mean wise, as when we say that the chairman of a meeting handled a tricky situation cleverly, or that a clever wife knows how to handle her husband.

These shades of meaning, however, can confuse the distinctions between various types of learning. There is the acquisition of 'pure' knowledge of facts, to memorize and to comprehend definitions, meaning and so on; and there is the ability to relate one piece of knowledge to another, how to generalize usefully from separate facts or theorize, or to reason from one set of facts to another. Part of the learning process is discovering how to use knowledge, how to develop theoretical or practical technique, how to adapt and apply what has been learnt. The commonly used term 'know-how' contains both features—knowing, and learning how to use knowledge. If we consider two very different examples we can see how widely (and, in the technical sense, often incorrectly) the word 'learning' is used.

The primitive hunter has to be shown how to use a spear and has practised using it. Imitation of more experienced hunters played a part in this process, but equally important has been his own practice, his own trial and error, by which he has become increasingly competent. In subtler ways he must have learnt a great deal of lore about hunting, the significance of sounds and scents, how to distinguise his approach and cover his tracks. His strength and skill are partly in-born, partly learnt and developed.

Similarly, an adult today faced with an unpleasant interview with a superior makes use of what he has learnt. He may be questioned about the actual job, to see if he has the facts about it at his finger tips. But he has also 'learnt' to deal with people, how to answer, how to ask, how to stand his ground, how to give way, how to convey what he wants to convey, how to respond to criticism. Much of this he will have 'learnt' without consciously realizing it; but, like the hunter, he has developed a complex skill (though a very different sort of skill) largely by trial and error.

Yet we are here describing a number of very different processes of 'learning'. We do not 'learn' to build up our personality pattern and reactions in the same way as we learn skills of (say) manual dexterity, or the fact that two and two make four. And in this chapter we are mainly concerned with what might be called 'academic learning'.

Why, then, in this area of learning, are certain people (and in particular children) quicker to achieve results? A number of important factors which modify, or damage this ability to learn are considered later in this chapter. But it must be emphasized here, that some important factors lie entirely outside the person concerned. All learning depends first on communication; or, in other words, on the various processes by which the information to be learnt is passed to, and received by, the learner. As we shall see later, the quality of the teaching and the relationship between teacher and taught are vital; but certain 'mechanical' factors are also involved. Severe deafness or total blindness are grave handicaps to normal processes of learning; but these are obviously and quickly recognized. What may be easily missed, but be almost as great a handicap to learning, are disabilities such as partial or temporary deafness or uncorrected errors of vision. The same is true of many other physical disabilities. All these factors must be looked for, or eliminated, when failures of learning appear.

There remains, however, one other vital factor which we have not yet considered—the intelligence level of the learner, and the essential differences between intelligence and acquired knowledge.

The scientific study of intelligence, the techniques of assessing it and the processes of learning fall within the province of the Psychologist (and in particular the Educational or Clinical Psychologist). As such, a detailed study of this topic is outside the scope of this book.[1]

Nevertheless, intelligence is one important facet of the total make-up of any individual. It is obvious that very low intelligence will be a considerable disability; and that this must have a marked impact on one's response to almost any situation; and, thus on both one's immediate emotional reaction and on one's total personality development. It is equally true, though less often appreciated, that high intelligence (or in certain circumstances even average intelligence) can have as great an impact on the total individual.

Equally, as we have already emphasized, the process of learning is not concerned only with the acquisition of factual information. To consider intelligence or learning without considering also the emotional implications of both, is to see

[1] Those readers who wish to go more deeply into the scientific and psychological aspects of intelligence and learning will find this concisely, but adequately, described in the appropriate chapter of *Child Psychology* by Prof. George G. Thompson, published by Houghton Mifflin Co., Boston, USA.

only part of the picture. Whilst, therefore, our main concern in this chapter will be on the emotional and clinical aspects, some simple explanations of intelligence and learning processes will also be necessary for a full understanding.

A simple definition of intelligence, which is reasonably accurate and quite adequate for our present purpose, is that it is 'the inborn capacity to learn from and through experience'. This definition contains two major premises on which there is some scientific dispute, but both are vital for an understanding of the broader emotional and personality aspects of the problem.

We are born with a certain 'quantity' of intelligence, a certain specific individual potential to be able to learn; and this quantity and potential remain virtually unchanged throughout life (except for the results of damage to certain brain cells due to disease, deterioration or injury).

The second premise, which must follow from the first, is the clear-cut distinction between our intelligence and what we learn. Thus, whilst it is true that the highly intelligent individual will be able to learn a good deal from any sort of experience, he is still dependent on that experience for the benefits of acquired knowledge and skills. It follows that for the less intelligent individual, more, and better, experience is necessary for adequate learning. The end-product—the knowledge and skills acquired—will be the combined product of intelligence and appropriate opportunities of learning.

In general terms it is true to say that our degree of basic intelligence not only offers us our potential to learn, but also sets the limits to what we are able to learn. The essential need, therefore, is to relate learning opportunity and methods, and the ultimate employment of our acquired skills in adult life to our own individual intellectual potential. A primary requirement for such a policy is an ability to assess with reasonable accuracy the basic intelligence of any individual.

Although we may condemn the examination system in detail (and especially perhaps its emotional aspects) it is a comparatively easy method of assessing the level reached by someone in acquired knowledge or skills. It is a much more difficult problem to assess accurately 'pure' intelligence. Virtually all forms of intelligence testing must rely to some degree on acquired skills or knowledge, for example, the ability to read, or to understand number work or to have undergone certain common experiences. Such factors are minimized, of course, in any adequate intelligence test; and attempts are made to concentrate on tests which demand basic reasoning ability rather than such acquired skills. (It is not suggested that reasoning ability is the sole factor in intelligence; but it is an important feature and it will serve here as an illustration.) Cultural and racial differences must also be considered in formulating any intelligence test.

In spite of, or perhaps because of, these difficulties, a very large number of different intelligence tests have been developed. These include tests suitable for the blind or the deaf or for those with other handicaps. Each test has its particular values and limitations so that the experienced clinical or educational psychologist will know which specific test is the most suitable for use in each different situation. For our purpose here, however, only two major classifications of tests are necessary, namely group tests and individual tests.

Most people are familiar with one or other of the numerous group tests, for these are used as part of the selective school examinations by many education authorities, or as an assessment procedure in some forms of professional or job selection. For our purposes the characteristics of a group test are that it can be given to any number of people at the same time; that the duration of the test as a whole is timed rather than the individual item; and that the test can be given and scored without specialist psychological skills being required. Such a type of test has obvious advantages; and where a large number of people need an intelligence assessment carried out under reasonably comparable conditions and in a short time, only a group test is practicable. But there are also appreciable disadvantages in this method. However hard the invigilator tries to produce the same environmental conditions for all the testees, a group test can make no allowances for individual differences in response to the test situation. However standardized the instructions are they can be individually misunderstood. Performance in such a test may be influenced by anxiety or by physical ill-health; but only the low performance and not the reasons for it will be apparent in the test score. Nor will the score differentiate between (for example) low scoring due to careless over-enthusiasm, to the unsure, too careful and too slow approach and genuine inability to perform the test. Group tests, when chosen and used appropriately, achieve a quite high degree of accuracy; and they probably represent the most reliable method we have at present for differentiating a large number of individuals into their appropriate levels of intelligence. But such tests cannot be, and indeed have never been claimed to be, 100 per cent accurate.

By contrast, and as the name implies, an individual type of test is given in a person to person interview. Such an individual test is a lengthy business; and such an interview cannot be rushed. Moreover whoever carries it out must be highly trained and professionally skilled in the use of test techniques. Ideally, and one might well say always, the tester should be a clinical or educational psychologist. The reason for this is not only that the whole test must be correctly and skilfully administered, important as this reason would be in its own right. But the psychologist will be trained, and able, to assess not only the test score and results, but also the testee's reaction to the test situation and to the tester himself. To name only a small number of factors, the speed of the response to each item of the test, the testee's anxious or over-confident response to both the whole test and to each item, and the differing 'successes' in the different parts of the test, will all give the psychologist valuable information. His report on the actual test interview, and on the differential breakdown between (say) the verbal and performance items of the test, will be quite as valuable and informative as the total test scores which he also produces.

Inevitably, therefore, an individual test will be more accurate in assessing intelligence than a group test can be; and it will give a much fuller 'picture' of the testee as a person.

No attempt will be made here to show how an intelligence test is validated and how the concept of mental age is arrived at. In very general terms, however, it is possible to say of any intelligence test which has been validated, that an average child of any given age should obtain such and such a total score. In reverse of this, therefore, if the testee obtains a given score on the test, we can say that his mental age is the age to which his score corresponds.

The concept of mental age taken by itself, is still sometimes used as a descriptive measurement of an individual's intellectual level; but it is a method which is subject to considerable objections. It is apt to give a picture of someone who is functioning on all respects at this age level; and this may well not be correct. Moreover, unless we know also the individual's actual chronological age (C.A.) to match against his mental age we have no indication at all of his relative intelligence in comparison with anyone else.

To avoid this latter difficulty it has been a popular practice to use as the unit of mensuration in this field the concept of intelligence quotient (I.Q.) which represents the relationship between mental and actual age expressed as a percentage:

$$I.Q. = \frac{M.A}{C.A.} \times 100$$

Some simple arithmetic will indicate the inherent value of this method. For it will be clear that if our M.A. and C.A. are the same, the I.Q. figure will be a hundred. But if the I.Q. figure is above a hundred the mental age is greater than the true age; if our I.Q. is below a hundred we have scored less than the average level for our age. We can say, therefore, even after only a quick glance at the I.Q. figure, that the individual concerned is of 'average intelligence'; or of above or below the average.

Yet there are serious objections to this form of descriptive measurement also. Although, therefore, 'I.Q.' has become a popular substitute in everyday speech for 'intelligence', many psychologists (and educational psychologists in particular) have largely given up the use of an intelligence quotient as a descriptive measurement of intelligence.

One obvious fallacy in this method of mensuration is that the concept of both mental and chronological ages must be modified to produce a valid I.Q. figure for an adult, as opposed to a child.

The strongest objection, however, stems from our basic attitudes towards the use of actual numerical figures in any scale of measurement. To quote an I.Q. of (say) 110 is to suggest a degree of mathematical accuracy and certainty which cannot be justified in practice. For example, if the same individual is given a number of different, although in their own way, equally valid and realiable tests the various I.Q.'s resulting from these various tests may vary by several points above and below a mean average figure. To take this even further, the actual I.Q. figures my vary within the separate sections of any one test; or between performance items or verbal items for example. An intelligence quotient figure quoted alone, and without reference to the specific test used, has little value; and could be misleading.

It has become customary in recent years, therefore, to refer to this intellectual level in much more general terms; and to describe someone as being of (say) 'superior intelligence', or 'on the borderline between average and above intelligence' and so on. Obviously the boundaries between these various levels of intelligence must be based on actual intelligence quotient figures; but the descriptive terms can be both more flexible and give a clearer picture of the individual's functioning level in the sphere of intelligence.

Important as it is to have some means of measuring and describing individual levels of intelligence, this must not blind us to the fact that such an assessment is not usually an end in itself, but rather a means to an end. We do not know a great deal about an individual if we consider only his intelligence, no matter how accurately this has been assessed.

Although the expressions are unscientific, it may be of considerable practical value to speak of an individual as 'using his superior intelligence very well', or of another, that he is 'duller than his intelligence test score would suggest'. Sometimes, of course, the detailed pattern of the individual items scored within the test itself indicate that the intelligence quotient is a measure of an individual's current functioning level rather than his true intellectual potential. Conversely, some adolescents with high scores on the verbal items in the test may appear much brighter and do better at school work (at least up to a certain point), than their average score on the total would seem to justify.

It is equally important to relate individual intelligence to levels of attainment in various specific subjects—which latter can be easily enough assessed. If, for example, we have a child of eight whose reading ability is only that of the average six-year old, all that we learn from this is that he is retarded in this subject by two years below his chronological age. But if we know that his mental age is also six years, then we will know that he is, in fact, functioning up to his real capacity; and that no amount of special reading help would appreciably raise his reading level or be justified. If, on the other hand, we find in similar circumstances, that the child's mental age is up to or above his chronological age, then we know that there is a true failure to function up to capacity. We can then seek the specific cause and provide the most suitable remedial help. Here, too, the internal pattern of the test scores may give us valuable pointers. Then, again, an individual test interview, conducted by an experienced practitioner, would distinguish here between the child whose attainments are retarded because he is anxious, and the child who is anxious because he is backward.

From such an illustration it will be clear that intelligence in its functioning results (as well as learning) are intimately linked to our emotional state and reactions. Thus, in quoting the intelligence level of any individual we are only describing one part, if an important part, of that individual's total make-up. His intelligence must always be considered alongside his maturity, his emotional stability, his physical characteristics, his personality, his use of his intelligence and so on. We must consider the whole person.

Learning is a very complex process. Although we know a good deal about such factors as motivation and incentives which promote (or inhibit) learning, we know comparatively little about the actual mechanics of the process within the brain. In this chapter, therefore, we are concerned only with a some-what simplified account of those aspects of learning which have special clinical significance.

'Learning' is used to cover a wide variety of activities. We learn to walk—and soon the complex techniques of walking becomes an automatic process which we can carry out without any conscious thought. Or, at the other extreme, we may undergo a whole series of minor, and sometimes even appar-ently unrelated, experiences, link these together and with the other pre-existing memories of earlier past experience, and from all these build up a new concept or idea or opinion.

Allowing for such differences as these, learning can be con-sidered as taking place in three stages.

Learning is not, as it is often commonly thought to be, merely a matter of taking in or absorbing facts or experience. That is only the first stage. The second is when this material is stored in the brain, through the complex and not yet fully understood mechanisms of memory. Third, we need to remem-ber, or recall, the material to consciousness. Perhaps it is not too fanciful to compare these three stages with a bank account. One makes the deposit or pays in, the money is stored or held, and it can usually be withdrawn on demand. The middle stage has nothing to do with us, that is the bank's part of it. Ours is to pay in and draw out. And we can only draw out after we have paid in; and then only if we use the right methods and follow the right rules for withdrawals.

We can influence very little the storage facilities of memory. Indeed our memory capacity, like our intelligence, is probably a fixed asset (or liability) modified only when some marked physical change occurs in our brain cells. But many factors can influence the first and third stages of the learning process, the taking in and the recall to conscious knowledge. It is an interesting illustration of this that when in ordinary conversa-tion we speak of someone having a good memory we usually mean that his recall processes are functioning well.

We are familiar with some of these influences from daily experience. We do not take in new knowledge, new facts, new names and dates and details effectively, nor do we remember

them so well if we are tired or distracted. If someone keeps talking to us or making a noise while we are trying to absorb something new, we complain that we cannot concentrate. Physical
conditions also make a difference. If we are too hot or too cold
or on an uncomfortable or too comfortable chair, or hungry or
thirsty or have a cold, it is more difficult to concentrate, to take
in new knowledge. Interestingly enough there are considerable
individual differences in what ruins or helps concentration in
different individuals.

Emotional factors also play a part. We cannot easily concentrate or recall if we are angry, sad, excited, dejected, anxious.
We complain that we 'can't keep our mind on the subject'.
This applies not only to learning something difficult that needs
prolonged attention but also to minor detail so that we seem
not to hear or to immediately forget, a simple request, a price
or a date, an address or a name. Such influences are usually
temporary and our ability to 'pay in' some new item will be
restored as soon as the emotional reaction has passed. Lack
of confidence also may affect us, as though we are feeling
'What's the use—I shall never remember all this'. So may over-
enthusiasm, when we rush at the material rather than attend
carefully to its detail. Other factors can have a more permanent
imfluence.

It is important to realize also that the emotional influences
need not always be present at the actual moment of absorbing
or bringing out the material. The emotional associations which
the material may have gained during storage, and of which we
are usually consciously quite unaware, can greatly influence the
process of recall. In ordinary parlance, we speak of something
'being too painful a memory for us to recall'.

Motivation (which is our own desire or otherwise to learn)
and incentives (which are the stimuli or inhibitions towards
learning which are provided for us by our environment) alike
play an important part in the learning process. Whilst this is
too large a topic to consider in detail here, one special feature
must be mentioned.

Perhaps the most important factor of all affecting the learning process is the nature of the relationship between teacher

and learner. A good deal that has to be learnt is mechanical, factual, informative, descriptive and the acquiring of techniques that do not have any special emotional content or significance. With this kind of learning the relationship between teacher and learner can affect the desire to learn, partly through 'catching' enthusiasm, partly through wishing to please the teacher in the way that the child needs to please his parents. There may also be some identification with a teacher who is liked and admired, so that the child wishes to emulate the teacher's ability. And unfortunately, all this can work the opposite way and become a disincentive if the teacher is disliked or despised. But if suitable teaching methods are used for this formal and factual work and if the motivation is adequate, the relationship between teacher and taught is only of limited importance. It is very different with other kinds of learning.

Much that has to be learnt (and not only at school or in childhood) is of emotional (rather than technical or factual) significance. It may be connected with emotional attitudes (as in history or drama) or belief (religion, philosophy, politics) or aesthetic feeling (the arts). In this area the nature of the relationship plays an important and sometimes decisive part. It is not so much what the teacher does but what he is, the kind of person he is and the kind of relationship he develops with the learners. The technical skill involved in this teaching has its value but without a positive personal relationship this emotional type of learning is almost impossible. One may learn trigonometry from a teacher one does not care about, but one will not learn to understand or appreciate poetry.

To the extent that learning is a part of emotional development, such factors as these are crucial. It is not only the subject that must really mean something to the teacher; the learners must also mean something to him, his relationship with them must be a real and positive one, with mutual feelings involved on both sides.

One is reminded here of what was said earlier about the absent parent. The presence of father or mother does not just mean being physically there; to be effective, it means also being emotionally committed to the child and to his well-being. And, although this relationship is significantly different, so it is with the teacher. The development of the personality is not just a matter of learning technical skills from parents and teachers. It is a matter of maturing emotionally, in relation with people who are deeply committed, not remote or inaccessible technicians. Learning in the full sense in which we have been considering it, is not simply a matter of what one learns to do. It is the kind of person one is becoming, also.

CHAPTER VII

The Impact of Change

Whether we like it or not, inevitably we shall be faced with the impact of changes in our environment. Such changes can (and will) occur at every stage of our life and development. Indeed, one measure of our successful maturation is the degree of success which we achieve in coping with such changes and adapting to them. For change is inevitably a source of stress to the organism.

We can see the pattern of this stress, and some of its results, by simple observation in our garden. If we transplant (say) a rose-bush from one place to another we know that we have to take special precautions if the bush is to 'take' successfully in its new plot. We know, too, that the plant takes some time to settle down and give of its best; and that if the change of environment is too great, and the stress too severe, then the plant may even die. But we can see also that if the new soil is better than the old, then our rose-bush will flourish. Thus, although changes in our environment produce stress, successful adjustment to the new environment means an important forward step. Indeed, if it were not for environmental changes and the organism's successful adaptation to them, no biological evolution of plants and animals could have taken place; and we, as human beings, would not exist.

Studies in the biological field illustrate another important aspect of the organism's adjustment to physical alterations in the environment. Many plants such as the desert cactus, for example, have complicated structures which enable them to survive in the dry, rainless atmosphere. We have elaborate inbuilt mechanisms which keep our body temperatures at a constant level whatever the weather; or which maintain our vital blood chemistry in balance. In other words, as far as physical changes are concerned, our body seeks to remain unchanged internally whatever alterations there may be in the environment.

80

Much of what we have said of biological changes can be applied to social and emotional changes in our life. These, too, produce stress for us. But maturity, mental health and security do not consist in avoiding stress, but in learning how to cope with it. We need, therefore, our own internal strength and defence mechanisms so that we can work through the changing situation without losing our own identity and so that we may gain from the new situation. We cannot escape the impact of change and the consequent degree of stress and difficulty. As the personality matures we learn how to adjust to new demands made on us by the environment, from changing conditions, from being transferred from one school to another, one job to another, one home to another, from joining fresh groups, meeting new people, entering a new phase of life, from getting married or retiring from work, from illness and holidays.

Some of these changes are wholly or partly of our own choosing, others are unavoidable. Some are accompanied by physical changes, others not. But we can divide such changes into two related, but nevertheless distinct, types.

It is simplest to study initially our reactions to types of change which are either of our own choosing or could only be avoided with difficulty. We could use as illustrations of this type such situations as a change from one job or school to another, or a move of house, or marriage or emigration.

If we study such changing situations in ourselves, or, better still, in others, we will see that we pass through three distinct stages of reaction.

First comes the stage of bewilderment when we (literally) do not know our way about in the new setting. Or, as we might put it, we do not know the new language. And, above all, we do not know when to ask and to whom we should turn.

Even in those instances when we wanted the change, applied for it and were delighted to move, the first phase is inevitably uncomfortable. We feel lost and bewildered. The old routine of getting to work and settling down among familiar work-mates— the journey that we could do almost with our eyes shut— had become a habit, but now we have to find the way, get used to a different route, adjust ourselves to a longer or shorter easier or more difficult journey, find how and where best to get a meal. We must get adapted to new people, new rooms, new conditions.

Obviously the more drastic the change (for instance, to a strange country or a completely different kind of job) the longer and more intense will be this first stage of bewilderment. Interestingly enough, however, very small changes in our environment can also produce a considerable phase of confusion, if for a rather different reason. If we move to the same job as our former one, but in a new firm, we somehow do not expect it to be different. Thus we are less prepared for those differences which are, in fact, inevitable.

Fortunately this uncomfortable phase rarely lasts long. It is familiar to us all and easy to recognize. What is less obvious and thus often takes us, and other people, by surprise, is the next stage, which has been called the negative phase.

In this, we had thought we were getting used to the new people and the new setting; but even so we are still uneasy or even resentful. In brief, we have not yet really accepted the new conditions. We begin to criticize some aspects of the new situation and tend to see the old one in a wistful, rose-coloured light. Now that (superficially) we have settled in and are less anxious about immediate details, we begin to see some snags. We wish ourselves back in our former environment. We tend to tell our workmates that in our old job, at our old firm, we did things differently and better. Naturally this does not make a very favourable impression on them and then we have something else to resent; people are not so friendly here as they used to be at our last job.

We are implying to ourselves and to others that this situation, these people, compare unfavourably with those we knew before and had got used to. Thus a vicious circle can quickly build up, in which we resent the new conditions and our new colleagues resent our fault finding. They feel we are disgruntled and we feel they are unfriendly and we continue to react on each other in this way. We feel we should not have made this change, it was all a mistake. Quite possibly we say so. Certainly we will feel so.

Clearly, this is not only a painful but a critical stage, both for us and for the new environment. We shall be strongly tempted to pack it in—and they to feel 'good riddance'. It is perhaps hardly surprising that some people actually do give up soon after changing to a new job or starting a new training or going for the first time to a university. There is, as we shall see towards the end of this chapter, a similar phase in most marriages also.

Sometimes the retreat from the new situation takes less obvious forms, particularly where an actual return is not possible. An immigrant who cannot go back home may be similarly unable to adapt himself to the way of life in his new surroundings. He may rigidly retain his original cultural pattern or even refuse to start learning the new language. There are more wistful ways of returning symbolically to old surroundings, the old regime, in re-union dinners, 'old boys' (and 'old girls') associations and in national societies (in foreign countries) where a cult of sentimental make-believe maintains the fiction of the old country, of home, where all was happy and secure, well-organized and familiar.

For immigrants to a new country there is also a counterpart of the workmates who resent the grumbling new-comer. Whole sections of a society, whole communities, can resent collectively the new arrivals. Serious social problems may arise from an influx of refugees or immigrants once the first phase has passed. For reasons which we have described criticism, hostility and resentment can become mutual. At the least, the newcomers complain that the hosts are stand-offish, boorish and unfriendly, if not actually hostile. And the hosts find plenty to complain of in the way the new-comers behave, the attitudes they adopt, because these are different from their own.

Fortunately with most of us in most situations this painful stage does not continue indefinitely. Most of us do not get beyond the stage of wishing ourselves back in the old environment. (Interestingly the time interval before we reach this wishful stage of retreat is remarkably constant for most people.)

Most of us, then, whatever we may wish to the contrary, continue to face up to the difficulties and gradually pass into the third stage, that of real adjustment. We now come to terms with both the advantages and the disadvantages of the new job, the new place, the new country. We may still sometimes compare it with the old, but we do so realistically, not with phantasies that all was bliss and sunshine and roses there. We can see now that some things are better here, some worse, and some just different. We have come to see our new environment (and the people in it) in a new light. We feel they have become more friendly (as indeed they may have). We are beginning to accept them realistically and they respond to the change in our attitude. We are now free to use the experience we gained in the old environment and adapt some of it for use in the new one. We can learn from mistakes we made there, so as not to repeat them here. In fact, we are now succeeding in adapting ourselves to the change. But it only begins after a period of distress and difficulty.

Just how long or severe these two first phases are (and whether we do pass successfully into the third stage of adjustment) will depend on many factors. Partly on how great the change is, how far-reaching the adjustment required of us, how different the new conditions from the old. Our own real motivation for making the change may make it easier for us to overcome the initial difficulties. If we came with others, with whom we can share our bewilderment and resentful feelings, we shall feel less lost and we may be helped, perhaps decisively.

Most of all, however, the outcome will depend on how successfully we have learnt to deal with environmental changes in the past. If we were helped to cope successfuly with the previous changes in our earlier life, if we did not run away from difficulty then, we shall be better able to deal with the present changes. We shall have more inner security, more confidence and more mature defences in adapting ourselves to new conditions.

Obviously, too, the child who has suffered from traumatic change in early life, before he was secure enough or mature enough to deal with these, may well be correspondingly handicapped in learning to adapt himself later. Equally if we have run away from difficulties and situations in the past, then the difficulties and fears towards any future new situation must appear larger than ever before; and thus much more difficult to face up to.

The second type of environmental change which we must now consider is the inevitable one. We cannot avoid moving into adolescence, or becoming middle-aged or old, however we may wish to do this, or try to do it in phantasy. We cannot even delay the onset of these phases.

Although these inevitable changes have much in common with our voluntary modifications of environment, they have certain special features of their own.

Their very inevitableness is a vital factor. But, in addition, every one of the four inevitable changes of life—the move from infancy to childhood, adolescence, middle-age and old-age— have three major features in common. Each change is spread over a long period, usually of several years duration. Each is linked and associated with equally inevitable and obvious bodily changes. And each demands completely new attitudes and expectations in ourselves and in those around us.

In recent years a mystique has grown up around the 'teen-age problem'. It has been so much publicised that one might even think that the problems of adolescence were somehow peculiar to the present era. So much is made of adolescent misbehaviour, it is such news, that to a considerable extent it may even increase the problem of both teenager and adult. Yet the criticism and hostility directed by adults at the adolescent are not at all new, nor are the adolescent's difficulties and responses. We need go no further back than reading the newspaper files of (say) thirty years ago to demonstrate this. And it was Keats who described adolescence as 'the space between (youth and childhood) in which the soul is in a ferment, the character undecided, the way of life uncertain'.

Contrary to what many people assume, or what we might presume from much of the publicity, the vast majority of adolescents of any generation are neither delinquent nor unstable nor promiscuous. Most of them sometimes find life difficult and problematical and most of them at times present a problem to their elders.

One can sum up the problem as the teenager sees it in those two so-often heard and contrasting phrases—'You are not old enough for that yet', and 'You are old enough to know better'. And although in a sense both are probably true, what is really being said, although not so often appreciated, is that the adolescent is neither a child nor an adult.

The problem as the parent sees it can be illustrated by the mother who tells her fourteen year old daughter, going out to her first 'date', that she must be home by half-past nine. The girl indignantly protests that she is no longer a child and her mother responds with 'It's just because you are no longer a child that I want you in by nine-thirty'.

The pattern of adolescence can be well illustrated by the story of the Garden of Eden—three things happened there, and these happen with the adolescent also. First there was the prohibition not to eat of the apple of knowledge—and the rebellion against this authority and this prohibition. In the long run the child accepts the authority of the adult; not always readily but nevertheless seeing its ultimate inevitability. But with adolescence, there comes a doubting of authority, a rebellion against it, a tendency to feel that any kind of adult authority must automatically be questioned. Their reaction may vary from frank rebellion to a sullen, resentful, disgruntled attitude to authority. Or they may think that they automatically know what is the right and proper thing to do, and that the grown-ups automatically are wrong in their ideas. This is a very difficult situation for the adult, particularly for the parent. There have been all those years from infancy through childhood when the child has been a child, and, on the whole, law-abiding and conforming. Then suddenly comes this adolescent throwing his (or her) weight about, arguing the point and being difficult or tiresome. It is easy for the parent or teacher to respond to this by trying to impose unsuitable authority; and this struggle can develop from a normal difficulty into a quite serious behaviour problem.

A second happening in the Garden was the seeking of new experience, the desire to eat the forbidden apple not merely because it was forbidden but to see what new experiences would follow. To the adolescent the world has suddenly expanded excitingly and dramatically, and there is a tremendous drive to explore this new world. They rush off into many new experiences and new activities with enormous enthusiasm, and as quickly change from one to another in a bewildering fashion. No sooner have the parents tried to provide for one interest than it is scrapped and something new is all the rage. This is one major factor behind the wastage of membership of youth clubs and groups. Many join on the crest of a new enthusiasm only to drift away to something else soon afterwards; or rush off eagerly to some new attraction. This seeking of new experience reinforces the rebellion against authority (as it did in the Garden of Eden). If a parent tells an adolescent to be home by ten, then five-past ten seems to be a world of new experience, something quite different in an exciting way, something that one wants to experience because it is new. As with the young child crawling across the floor towards the fire, the parent knows that the adolescent has not the experience to keep all his enthusiasm within bounds and to judge adequately. And so the parents inevitably become rather anxious and worried about the outcome; and unsure how to protect the adolescent from his own enthusiasm.

Thirdly there is the physical development of puberty—the realization by Adam and Eve of their own nakedness. Adolescence is a time of great physical growth and physical change, each very obvious and partly exciting and partly frightening. This again is a new experience that he must explore. But his interest in this new world of feeling, associated with sexual development, is coloured by the general attitudes of those adults around him that it is something dangerous or bad. Many adolescents feel torn between the urge to explore this stimulating, powerful and exciting new feeling, and the prohibitions of the controlling mechanism within and the outside influences from their parents or teachers. The adolescent is in a difficult situation here. Physically he is an adult, and perhaps economically too if he has started work; but in terms of social development he cannot yet possibly act as a mature adult. If he is still at school, or is a student, he is still treated in many respects as a child, despite his 'adult' attributes. And so we have a good deal of confusion surrounding him—in some ways he feels more grown up, in others less so. There is therefore inevitably a good deal of anxiety aroused by all this uncertainty and by these far-reaching changes.

Perhaps we can put all this in terms of another analogy. It is as though throughout childhood, the boy or girl has been living in a walled garden. It is in many ways a pleasant place, with plenty to do in it and plenty to explore. It is reasonably well protected from dangers of every kind and there are a pair of reasonably beneficent guardians to set things right if they go wrong. After a dozen years or so the child has got to know this garden well and to feel at home, though perhaps a little bored, in it. Then one day he discovers a gate in the wall which he had not seen before. He opens this, and looking out he sees a new and exciting world. He at once begins to feel he is tired of the garden he knows so well and longs to go out to explore the new world outside it. That is very much the situation of the adolescent. Sometimes they venture out a little, but keep (as it were) one eye on that garden gate so they can go back inside if necessary. In this way, looking back over their shoulders, they do not always see where they are going and bump into things, or hurt themselves. Sometimes they suddenly catch sight of something new and exciting and go rushing off after it, regardless of the obstacles or dangers in the way. Then, perhaps they lose their nerve or hurt themselves and dash back temporarily into the garden again for safety.

It is important to appreciate that adolescence is a difficult period for the adults concerned also. They have to learn to give up something that is of value to them, their parent-child relationship. It is understandable that as parents we should want to prolong this a little. It is as difficult sometimes for the parents as it is for the adolescents to adapt themselves to the new relationship of parent-adolescent. That, in its turn too, will have to be outgrown to be replaced by the relationship between adults, between parent and grown-up son or daughter.

The role of the adult during the process of adolescence is still one of control, but of a new sort of control; of helping the young person to grow through the difficult stage without getting too much hurt in the process. An incident described by a father will illustrate one of these points. He had just returned home from work as his adolescent son came out on his bicycle. As the boy rode away he called out cheerily 'How do, old cock?' The father was horrified for a moment, so taken aback that he had no reply. But as the boy rode out of ear-shot, his mind already on what he was going to do, his father realized that really, in a way, this adolescent was suddenly treating him as one of his friends. There are often shocks of this kind and difficult patches as parent and son or daughter pass from one kind of relationship into another. But the process has its rewards, too, for both of them.

As we have noted, adult society as a whole tends to be critical of (and even hostile to) the adolescent. The reasons for this adult attitude are complex and we have studied some of the factors involved already. But two other factors illustrate normal mental mechanisms in operation. To the adult the adolescent growing into manhood or womanhood is a threat—and a reminder that we are no longer so young and able to compete ourselves. As a result we may either try to pretend (without much success as a rule!) that we can compete with youth at its own game. Or, more commonly, we condemn in the adolescent those activities which unconsciously we would like to emulate, but which we cannot admit to ourselves openly. As well as this, many adults genuinely find it difficult to remember the details of their own adolescent activities, for we tend to repress out of memory situations which were, at the time, stressful or guilt-provoking to us.

Two other important aspects of adolescence require consideration. We all know of (and most usually condemn and criticize) the 'pashes' of the adolescent—those intensely emotional, close, dependent attachments that the teenager makes with an older person of the same sex. Yet these serve to remind us that the normal adolescent passes through a normal stage of homosexual attraction in the move towards ordinary adult heterosexual relationships. In a way this is a repetition, or continuation, of the process we saw in infancy, the need to model oneself on an adult of the same sex with whom one has a close, warm and secure relationship. And, as with other relationships, the results of this contact at this stage will depend on the 'success' of those earlier relationship patterns in infancy. If this foundation was soundly based, then this adolescent relationship can be used constructively; but where there has been no adequate parental relationship, the impact of a 'bad' adult figure in adolescence can be disastrous.

It will be obvious that individual and cultural differences of experience and opportunity will influence the widening social contacts of the adolescent, but it is surprising how frequently these follow the same general pattern of development. It is by no means uncommon to see three stages following one another. In the earlier years of the period the characteristic social group is a small homogeneous one, all of the same sex and age. This will gradually change into the small group of both sexes. And only beyond this stage is it common to see the same boy and girl regularly together and away from the group for any length of time. And, surprisingly often, the first chosen individual partner will be picked from outside the original group.

For the majority, another major change occurs during this period of emotional confusion and stress—leaving school and starting work. It is perhaps sufficient commentary on this to say that society is likely to expect 'grown-up' behaviour and responsibilities from the fifteen-year old who has left school, and to treat the next-door teenager who is still at Grammar School as a child. Yet this further move into the outside world, and the new independence which it provides, will set complex adjustment difficulties for both adolescent and parents.

How, then, do we, as the parent or other adult concerned, handle this stage? How do we help the adolescent to work through this phase and emerge as a mature adult with the maximum degree of security and the minimum risk of being badly hurt or going astray during the intervening period of development? There are the two possible extremes of adult reaction which we have already mentioned, but which must be considered in more detail here.

We can continue to treat our teenager as though he were still a child, either in the sense that we try to overprotect him from any contact with the 'dangerous' new world into which he is growing; or by continuing to impose the same controls and prohibitions and exert exactly the same sort of authority as we did when he was a small child. The dangers of such a course are obvious.

Yet the other extreme, of assuming that the teenager is capable of adult decisions and of setting all his own standards for himself (a much more common extreme nowadays) has equally great dangers; and it sets very severe problems for all concerned.

If we turn again to our analogy of the garden of childhood, would it not be wiser if the gate from the garden led not into the big wide outside world, but into an area of parkland—an area much bigger than the original garden and containing the means and opportunity for many new activities, adventures and discoveries; but an area still surrounded by a wall which has the double function of enabling the teenager to 'experiment' safely within a wider life and indicating clearly to him where the boundaries of acceptable exploration and behaviour lie?

In brief, the adolescent still needs an adult who will firmly and confidently set and maintain reasonable boundaries of acceptable behaviour yet allow reasonable freedom within these boundaries. Without such understanding yet confident adult control the teenager will be insecure and unhappy; and he will find it hard to complete the change into adulthood without distress or disaster—or both. Indeed a great deal of provocative adolescent behaviour, including such dramatic episodes as running-away from home, can be a cry for help and an attempt to discover where the boundaries of acceptable behaviour, so far not demarcated for them, stand. Those with long experience of working with difficult adolescents will confirm how much more settled and happy these teenagers become in a more consistently handled environment such as we have described.

It is not easy, of course, for the parent or adult to decide upon these standards and set them out confidently for the adolescent. Adult society as a whole is tending to question those ethical standards which it formerly accepted automatically. With some, the 'cult of liberalism' is carried to a degree which is entirely unrealistic for any sort of ordered community. Commercial pressure and advertising technique, specifically directed towards the now relatively 'well-off' adolescent group, may exploit very different standards from those the average parent (or, for that matter, the average adolescent not subject to such pressures) would wish to accept. Finally, of course, the shrewdest of manipulation will be used by the adolescent to play such varying standards off against each other and to produce much uncertainty, if not guilt, in the parents' mind. After all, if our thirteen-year old daughter says indignantly 'It's not fair; all the girls in my class'—by which incidentally she means two or three of the girls—'wear nylons. Why can't I?', it is difficult for the good parent not to feel unreasonable! Yet, in the long run, such decisions must be made and such standards set in important as well as small matters by the adults themselves. We shall not help the adolescent by being only condemnatory or critical. But we shall equally not be helpful if we are too 'starry-eyed' about them.

The adolescent, of course, begins to question adult authority just at a time of life when the parents themselves are beginning to feel insecure. They are, in fact, facing or moving into a stage of change in their own development that has many parallels to adolescence itself. A new world is opening before the adult, too, which they may not welcome but which they cannot avoid. Their powers and abilities begin to show at least some signs of waning. Physical changes appear also, the middle-age spread, baldness, somewhat impaired concentration, dexterity and stamina not quite what they were. The middle-aged man may well have reached his vocational ceiling. The woman may feel past her best in appearance and attractiveness and the change of life will remind her that her period of child-bearing is at an end. It is hardly surprising that they tend to resent any questioning of their status and authority. Just as the adolescent needs to start questioning authority, the parents may feel the need to preserve it. Both are feeling insecure under the impact of change—physical, emotional and social.

And so, both the adolescent and the adult facing middle age, show the response to change which we described earlier in this chapter—bewilderment, criticism and counter-criticism and finally adaptation.

The basic reactions to the other two inevitable changes have much in common with those which we have described for adolescence and middle age.

The infant moving into childhood during the four to six-year old stage is faced with many stresses both physical and social. He loses his babyish physique, he has to learn, and to adjust to, new physical skills and activities. The expectations made upon him (and to some extent his expectations for himself) alter greatly. And he has to make the major social adjustment of beginning at school. It is not surprising that he may be often reluctant to make this onward step and that he may show evidence of insecurity, and even anxiety, during the period of change.

Both the adolescent and the middle-aged, once they have successfully adjusted to and completed the change, move into relatively calmer waters. Like the man who had adjusted to his new job, they can now use their past knowledge and experience constructively in their new setting. For the child who has successfully passed beyond infancy, however, this phase of relatively quiescent behaviour is particularly striking; and it is dignified with the descriptive label of 'latency'. Moreover this latent phase is of vital importance, for it covers the period of maximum learning and maximum physical growth for the child. Thus once again we can see how failure to cope with change will not only affect the quiescent stage which should follow, but may well damage the important development that should take place during that quiet stage.

The final inevitable change of life, the move into old age, has special features of its own. The signs of physical deterioration, however slowly these appear, are severe, very obvious and unavoidable and, most important of all, non-reversible. However much a man may welcome, or dislike, retirement from his work, it requires a major readjustment in his whole way of life. By the very nature of things many of his friends and contemporaries will be dead; and he may have few, or none, of his own family around him. Last, but by no means least, he sees himself as moving towards the end of life. This can well be the most difficult of all the changes of life to cope with. Indeed, it would probably always be the worst if it were not that the very fact of our slow deterioration prevents us from feeling it as acutely as we otherwise might.

One major adjustment which we all have to make is in our growing and changing relationship with the opposite sex, and particularly in the realm of boy- (or girl-) friend, of engagement and marriage.

The passionate idealism of adolescence gradually colours his relationships with the other sex. To the biological aspects of adolescence is added a complex emotional one, partly affection and partly idealism or phantasy. The young adult begins to experience an intense need for an exclusive relationship with the one person, a 'grown-up' and much more complicated version of his infantile relationship-needs.

This relationship will be something unique in his experience and in that sense we are justified in regarding it as another, though very special, change that makes a great impact on him. (This may seem a gross understatement of the experience of falling in love but, as we shall shortly see, it is at least partially valid.)

It is reasonable to recognize that the intense impact of this experience shows many of the characteristics of other personal change. We described the first phase as being (mainly) bewilderment. Certainly the lover and beloved experience a sense of confusion, delicious though it is. They feel in a different world, everything feels different in some unaccountable way—yet in another sense it is not unaccountable. One is bewilderingly transported as a child at a party or on Christmas morning, yet this is a fuller experience, more absorbing and exclusive.

The second negative stage has its parallel too in the 'lovers' quarrel', those particularly painful misunderstandings that one so deeply resents. The loved one seems suddenly to fail our ideal; we feel betrayed and we are hurt and angry. We may be astonished that we deliberately hurt the person who means most to us. Sometimes our relationship does not survive this stage and we cut adrift from one another, like the worker who cannot adapt himself to the new job.

When we get married, we again find these characteristics of major change. The first bewildering stage passes into one where we begin to find fault, to criticize, to compare unfavourably, to feel let-down, to see our old life through rose-coloured glasses. Only gradually (and sometimes quite painfully) do we reach the stage of acceptance and adaptation. Sometimes people are unable to reach it and after only a few months or years of marriage, escape out of it back to their old way of life. Sometimes, the same sequence is then repeated. Sometimes, an adaptation is only partly reached. These processes are immensely complicated because two people are mutually involved and because many of the issues are not fully conscious. The task of helping people to pass from a hostile phase to the stability of acceptance and adaptation is a long and difficult one, requiring a special kind of skill.

A further milestone in a life of changes occurs when a marriage becomes a family. The role of wife becomes also the role of mother, bringing fundamental changes for both wife and husband. Once again the initial bewildering excitement will pass into a negative phase. Sometimes one or other partner cannot get beyond this but retreats out of it and the marriage is threatened or broken. More often (with or without skilled help) this phase is surmounted and a new era opens in which both husband and wife accept the re-orientation of their family life and of their individual roles within it and in society.

And then, still later, comes the adolescence of the children and the middle age of the parents. There are now emotional echoes of the time they first had a child. They have grown used to having their children around but now they have this adolescent, who is not quite a child nor adult. They are faced once more with the family triangle in a new form. Once more there are sexual overtones to the new relationships that are emerging. There is a different kind of challenge between an adolescent son and father on the one hand and his mother on the other. This sometimes precipitates difficulties between the parents, often as

95

intense as the comparable difficulties which arose when the child was first born. At a reality level, no less than at an unconscious level, the sexually mature adolescent has a role vis-à-vis one parent quite different from his relationship to the other. Indeed, adolescent brother and sister often notice how sharply the family relationships can become differentiated, the daughter on edge with mother, the boy with father.

Other inescapable changes follow. The husband retires from active work, young people marry, there may be illness, disablement or bereavement, and perhaps a grandparent comes to live in the home. All deeply significant changes makes an impact on us; and the way we respond gives a measure of our maturity. We share this impact as a part of our personal destiny, and by our reactions we help or hinder those who are closest to us as they try to reach a satisfactory and satisfying adjustment.

CHAPTER VIII
Body and Mind

Scientific medicine has given many and obvious benefits to mankind. But the pattern of its development delayed for many years any real understanding of psychiatric illness. To some degree this pattern still delays a full acceptance of the close and constant inter-relationship between emotional and physical factors. In the pre-scientific day, when medicine had not really divorced itself from magic, this interconnection was easier to accept, even though that acceptance was largely based on ignorance. (It is interesting to speculate, however, how many of the phenomena of 'possession' or of physical damage produced by spells described in the mediaeval witchcraft trials could now be explained in the light of advancing scientific knowledge.)

It was natural and inevitable that bodily symptoms should first and mainly occupy the interest of the doctor, whilst the developments in the sciences of pathology, pharmacology and physiology strengthened the emphasis on the concept of an organic bodily cause for all ill-health. The emphasis in professional training was on the abnormal; and on the diseased or damaged organ rather than on the patient as a person. The good clinician still retained some personal contact with his patient, but the greater the dependence on laboratory and similar diagnostic methods and the greater the degree of specialization within medicine itself, the harder it became to retain this clinical contact with the patient as a whole person.

For many years, and indeed until comparatively recently, the study of emotional disturbance and mental illness lagged far behind the progress of general medicine. Successful forms of treatment were virtually non-existent and little was known of the causation of these disturbances and disorders. The literature on this subject tended to concentrate on detailed clinical description of specific patterns of symptoms and on the clinical diagnosis of various types of mental illness. Many of these descriptive writings reached the same high standard as had the similar obervational description of physical ailments in the period immediately preceding that of scientific medicine. Each type of clinical descriptive writing had demanded the same closer observation of the patient as an individual and therefore some concern with the patient as a person.

Three major lines of development have revolutionized this situation in this century. Whilst it is true that the beginnings of these new lines of discovery did not coincide exactly in time, their further development and wider acceptance have over-lapped to a significant degree. The work of Freud, Jung, Adler and many others who have followed them opened up entirely new concepts in the understanding and treatment of emotional disorders. A beginning, and a very significant beginning, was made in the study of brain physiology and function. New physical and pharmacological techniques revolutionized the treatment (in every sense of that word) of the mentally sick. All three were vital and valuable moves forward; but taken together they have produced their problems. Of the three, only one (the study of brain neuro-physiology) could stand up to the rigorous and specific demands of scientific proof. Psychopatho-logical theory, however validated in clinical study and practice, does not lend itself readily to those statistical or experimental studies which are the hall-mark of pure scientific investigation; and although much pharmacological research lies behind the development of new drugs for use in mental ill-health, the knowledge as to why these forms of treatment are successful remains largely empirical. This lack of scientific proof as between various new approaches made controversy almost in-evitable between the adherents of each different theory. This, of course, was unfortunate in itself; but such controversy also widened the split between the physical and emotional aspects of causation and treatment in these disorders.

Yet, in fact, these varying advances in knowledge are com-plementary to each other rather than in rivalry. It is not (or should not be) a question of debating whether the physical or the emotional factor is the more important in any given situation or reaction. What is much more important is to appreciate that these two factors can never be entirely separated. Each must interact with the other, in every situation of life. One may stress (as we do in this book) the psychological factors, the way the individual feels, the impact of his feelings on his behaviour, the response of others to this reaction and how they feel in this situation. But this behaviour and response involves not only emotional and mental mechanisms. Always these will require for their production some change in bodily functioning, or some similar bodily change will follow inevitably. Even thinking and feeling involve electro-chemical activity within the brain cells. If a drug is administered to relieve pain or reduce anxiety, this physical method of treatment affects how the patient *feels* about his illness. In turn this will have its repercussions on his family and those close to him also. The reverse is equally true, as is illustrated by the old medical jest that if an injection of morphia is the correct treatment for certain forms of haemorrhage, then it will be most effective if given to the relatives rather than to the patient! Every emotion therefore has its associated bodily responses and mechanisms; and we will have some emotional reaction to every physical ailment or change in bodily functioning. There can be no such thing as a purely physical illness or a wholly psychological disturbance. We cannot divorce psyche and soma no matter how convenient it might sometimes be to do so.

The description of many of our bodily responses to emotion has passed into everyday speech. We talk of being 'sick with apprehension' or 'hot with anger'; of the 'sinking feeling' that accompanies fear. Some years ago a film was made of a group of medical students awaiting their turn to go into an oral examination. The film was made without their knowledge. Of this group a number are to be seen walking up and down purposelessly and restlessly, some are wiping the perspiration from their brows or palms, whilst others try to wet their dry lips or to swallow their saliva much more vigorously than usual. During the few minutes of filming one or two students make their way to the nearest lavatory.

These students are showing some of the normal bodily 'symptoms' of normal anxiety. In addition to these visible symptoms, some might have complained of a tightness in the chest, or of palpitations or of digestive symptoms. If we had medically examined the students, we might well have found a general, if usually small, increase in pulse rate, dilation of the pupils and other signs of changing physical function.

This same concept can be illustrated equally clearly from our own personal experience of our bodily reaction to (say) a sudden fright or to an outburst of anger. Although we find that any one bodily response can result from more than one emotion, each emotion has its own particular bodily reactions which are specific to that emotion. Even so, as the group of medical students demonstrated, each individual tends to 'select' (not by conscious choice but possibly for constitutional reasons) certain responses which will tend to predominate whenever he is faced with that particular emotion.

Basically all these physical responses to emotional stimulus have a biological purpose. If we are afraid, then our body responds in the way which will best prepare us for physical 'flight'; our response to anger raises our bodily efficiency towards the possibility of 'fighting'. In the animal kingdom the value of such response is obvious. With civilized man the disadvantages of such bodily responses may often outweigh the advantages. Yet these responses are automatic and entirely outside our conscious control. It is this inevitability which is responsible for some, at least, of the disadvantages and dangers. For our palpitations, our hot flushed skin, the tightness in our chest or whatever the symptoms may be, are not imaginary, but are the result of actual changes in our bodily functioning. As such, and because we rarely recognize for ourselves the cause of these changes, it is easy and common for us to mistake these normal reactions for the symptoms of actual bodily illness—and from this fresh emotional symptoms may arise.

This pattern of interaction can be most vividly observed in some of the so-called psychosomatic illnesses—so-called since the thesis of this present chapter is that *all* ill-health is basically psychosomatic. Asthma will serve as a good example, however, of an illness where both psyche and soma are very clearly involved and interrelated.

In this condition, periodic attacks occur in which the small air passages of the lungs become constricted so that the patient has great difficulty in getting air in or out of his chest. An attack of asthma is a disturbing and even frightening experience both for the sufferer and for the onlooker. On this ground alone there would be obvious emotional implications to this bodily disease. But the interaction goes deeper also. It has long been known that attacks of asthma were produced by the patient's exposure to certain specific substances—dust or the hair of a particular animal for example. The patient is allergic (as they say) to this particular material so that contact with it sets up a complex series of chemical reactions within the body which result in the spasm of the air passages—and the attack of asthma. But it is also known that this same chain of chemical reaction, and therefore an attack of asthma, can result from purely emotional causes. The patient may *think* that he is exposed to dust (or whatever his allergic substance is); and the consequent fear that an attack is imminent and inevitable may well produce, unaided, such an attack. Nor is this in any way an imagined attack. The spasm of the small passages is there, and with this all the resulting symptoms. Indeed the attacks will be indistinguishable from each other unless we can ascertain from the history whether it has been produced by physical or emotional factors. Most sufferers from asthma will have both types of attack; and many of their attacks will be of mixed causation.

Two important conclusions can be drawn from the example of this illness. Although death is fortunately an uncommon result of asthma, it can occur; and very often serious physical damage to the structure of the lung will follow long-continued and frequent attacks. Consequently it is perfectly possible for actual lung damage, or even death, to result from causes which, initially, are purely emotional. What is of even greater practical significance, however, is the very obvious need to consider both the emotional and physical needs of the patient in parallel and equally. It is as purposeless to treat *only* the bodily symptoms and disability as it would be dangerous to concentrate solely in the psychological factors and ignore the physical.

If this inter-relationship is most vividly seen in asthma, or in one of the other 'psychosomatic' illnesses, this should not blind us to the same, if lesser, degree of interaction in every type of illness.

If one has an ordinary cold, for example, part of the typical reaction is physical, but part is also emotional. One feels sorry for oneself; and one tends to concentrate on one's symptoms at the expense of other interests and activities. To some degree one becomes more self-centred than usual.

If the illness is more severe, and especially if it is prolonged or disabling, these characteristic reactions become more marked. At first the patient may fight hard to face up to his illness; and obviously different people give way in differing degrees. Inevitably, however, more and more concentration will fall onto our symptoms; and whilst our emotional reaction will normally begin as anxiety, long continuing anxiety is so difficult to bear that we may try to cover our anxiety by what becomes almost pride in our symptoms. Or, at very least, it becomes a need to stress our symptoms to ourselves or to others. It can be a considerable relief to our anxiety if we can talk about our difficulties and symptoms.

Similarly our initial, and sometimes considerable, anxiety about what is happening to our family or our job whilst we are ill may become so overwhelming and insoluble that we may have to drive this underground also. The unavoidable sense of isolation of being in bed, or in hospital, has its obvious results here also. When our visitors come the tendency is for our ailments and our own limited activities to take precedence in the conversation over whatever news they bring us from the outside world.

This retreat into, and involvement with, our own illness accentuates our degree of disablement; and accentuates too our inevitable feeling of dependence on others. For what is probably the first time since childhood, the patient has to rely wholly on others for his comfort, his well-being and for the very necessities of life. If his illness is very severe he may need to return to the completely infantile state of being washed and fed. It is not surprising, therefore, that sooner or later, and to some degree at least, every one of us when ill will regress emotionally also into a more childlike, more immature, pattern of reaction and feeling. (It is an interesting speculation as to how far this inevitable regression influences the traditional attitudes of the medical and nursing professions towards the patient; and how far this in turn accentuates and increases that degree of regression and dependence.)

During the course of a prolonged or serious illness such a regression into self-interest, self-pity and willing dependency can be a valuable, and on the whole useful, defence mechanism. The difficulties arise as we recover from our illness and have to 'grow up' again. For 'growing up' and physical recovery can easily get out of step with one another. There tends too often to be too sharp and sudden a line drawn between illness and recovery.

For recovery, however much it may be welcomed for other reasons, leaves us no longer the focus of so much care, attention and interest. It forces us to face up once more to the problems and demands of the outside world. Such a process will take time, and help, to achieve. Thus recovery and rehabilitation need to be as skilfully and carefully planned as does the treat-ment of the disease itself. Yet there are powerful and under-standable reasons why this is difficult to ensure. By the tra-ditional pattern of their training, the medical and nursing pro-fessions concentrate much of their skill and knowledge—and therefore their interest also—on disease rather than on health. As the patient recovers from his illness the pressure on nurse or doctor will be to transfer attention to some new sick person. Our hospital bed may be needed urgently for another patient, but it is difficult for the patient to accept this transition at a few hours' notice from being the invalid in hospital to coping with the outside world again. Our relief and pleasure at re-covery will be mixed with both anxiety and uncertainty. We may try to cope with this too sudden step to re-maturation by a desperate attempt to become entirely well too quickly. Or, perhaps more commonly, we may cling to our residual symptoms even to the point of chronic invalidism.

The degree to which this 'growing up' again presents a prob-lem depends not only on the help which physical and emotional rehabilitation techniques can give. It is a highly individual matter also; and related closely to our personality pattern and past life experience and to what the actual illness meant to us socially and emotionally.

Did we see our illness as a safe and secure escape from the stresses of life; or as a 'weapon' which gave us sympathy, understanding or power which we had not found when well? Did we feel ill-health as a threat to our security and to our ability to earn our living and support our family; or with a sense of failure on our part at being ill, however unjustified this fear may be in reality? Had anyone explained our illness to us and discussed its implications for full recovery or residual disability? Had we been treated in hospital as a 'complete' person, or as 'the case in bed 14' or 'the broken leg'? All these, and other similar factors, will influence our basic attitude both to the illness, and, especially, to the period of recovery.

True malingering is uncommon. But there are very few of us who have not at some time dramatized our symptoms or used them to our own advantage; or on other occasions minimized our symptoms because of our anxiety.

Obviously, therefore, our reaction to our own illnesses will be individual to us; but there are some specific disabilities which produce a characteristic emotional response from us even if we are not sufferers ourselves. Total blindness in another person will provoke intense sympathy and a very protective attitude in us. We do not make jokes about the blind; and we are ready to subscribe to organizations whose aim is their care. Contrast our attitude to total deafness, which is an equally severe disability. We are likely to make far fewer allowances for the deaf; and we may be irritated by, or even make fun of, his difficulties in communication. Whatever the deeper emotional reasons for this difference, it is clear that our differing attitudes must have considerable impact on the feelings and reactions of the sufferer himself towards his disability.

It is perhaps understandable that we dread cancer as one of the killer diseases; but the fear that we *might* have cancer can produce intense anxiety for us. Our fear may drive us into hiding our symptoms rather than seeking medical advice for them on the entirely illogical, but common, fallacy of the ostrich who buries his head in the sand.

Nor is our dread of particular diseases always founded on medical fact. St Vitus Dance is nowadays an uncommon disease in children; yet it is still greatly dreaded. The parents whom we can convince that their child does not have this disease will be greatly relieved even when our actual diagnosis is of a medically much more serious condition. In many parts of the country tuberculosis is still viewed as a disease of dirt and poverty and a condition which the sufferer must feel ashamed to have. Once again such fixed attitudes must influence how the patient feels about his disease; and how we feel about the sufferer.

Epilepsy will serve as a good example of how all these complex reactions and feelings can influence the total development of the individual's personality. In this condition the fits usually begin at a very early age. The major attacks of unconsciousness vary greatly in frequency; and above all, these attacks are unpredictable in their onset. At most the patient may have a very brief warning. More often there will be no warning before he falls unconscious to the ground. This must not only be anxiety-provoking for the patient and those in whose care he is; it must place many inevitable restrictions on his activities. He cannot swim, or climb or ride a bicycle or drive any vehicle. He must be kept from situations where such a sudden fall might be dangerous. If he has injured himself in a previous attack he will tend to be watched with anxious protectiveness. In these circumstances it will be difficult for the child to mature, to gain confidence and skills from new situations or experiences. It will be easy for him to remain at a self-centred, attention-demanding infantile level of reaction. His social contacts and relationships will suffer also for he may be ostracized by those who dread seeing his attacks, or treated with elaborate pity or anxious protectiveness. Either way it will be difficult for him to form the secure and gradually maturing relationships which he needs if he is to build up any adequate personality strength. Nor is epilepsy a disease of limited duration. It is often, although not always, possible to reduce the incidence of the fits; but it is rarely that the patient can be given a definite reassurance that the fits will never recur.

In a condition such as this we can see, and accept, the impact of bodily illness and emotional reactions upon each other; and the influence that this can have on the progress of the physical disease and on the patient's personality. On many other occasions this inter-relationship will be less clearly seen. Yet, if we neglect this inter-relationship and fail to contend with both the emotional and the physical we cannot hope to understand, let alone help, the sick or emotionally disturbed individual.

But in all this we must remember another important factor, the narrow border-line between health and illness; and with this the danger of hypochondriasis by too much concentration on health.

On medical grounds it might be justified to advise periodic regular medical 'check-ups' for all. Certainly there would be very few doctors who would not say that early diagnosis is esential for success in treatment; and advise, therefore, that if one has a serious symptom one should seek medical advice at once. Yet in certain circumstances may not this produce an unnecessary dread of disease; and an undue concentration on our symptoms rather than on our 'positive' health?

We can illustrate this same problem in a rather different, but very common, situation.

The pregnant mother will have, and indeed must have for her own protection, a considerable concentration of care, attendance and examination by the doctor and his colleagues in the allied professions. It will be emphasized how important it is for her to attend the Ante-Natal Clinic; she may be advised to have her baby in hospital. She will receive a great deal of advice on the care of her health, on her diet, on the techniques of muscular relaxation and so on. Such preventive medicine policies have enormously reduced the figures of maternal and infantile mortality; and equally reduced the chronic ill-health which can follow pregnancy and childbirth. But will it be easy for this expectant mother to see the whole business of child-bearing as a normal biological process?

But there is another side to this same coin. A good deal

of health education in the post-war years has gone to emphasize the 'normality' of pregnancy and child-birth. Yet even the most 'healthy' mother will have some distressing symptoms and some physical handicaps, at least during the later stages of her pregnancy. Some mothers can become puzzled, or even anxious, when faced with these apparent contradictions. She may be tempted to overdrive herself, to feel that she ought not to have such symptoms with such a normal process.

It is worth remembering therefore that our emotional attitudes can be linked to health as well as to ill-health.

CHAPTER IX

The Family and the Wider Social Environment

One could suppose that the field ornithologist is sometimes a little jealous of his botanical colleagues in that whilst the latter can spend what time he chooses to study the detailed structure of a flower, birds rarely stand still long enough for him to be certain whether they have a scarlet beak, or pink legs or whatever identifying features are important. Human beings are rather like birds in this respect; for they, too, rarely 'stand still' for long enough for prolonged study.

For one of the major difficulties in the accurate study of human behaviour is that man's reactions and behaviour are not something static and unchanging. As has been stressed throughout this book, his responses to any single situation is individual to him and to that particular situation. However, since the situation itself is dynamically and constantly changing through the reactions of all the other people who are also involved, even this individual response must be fluid and dynamic and constantly and equally responsive to the changing situation. To put this problem in another way, we have to consider and observe the individuality of each human being whilst appreciating that he does not, and indeed cannot, exist in a vacuum but only as part of a complex web of dynamic, constantly changing and inter-acting human relationships.

It is inevitable, therefore, that human behaviour is governed by an almost unlimited number of variables. It is this variability that limits research within the social sciences; and which produces vital differences between these fields of research and those in the physical sciences. For example, it would not be difficult to set up a carefully controlled experiment which might show (say) that adolescents in a co-educational grammar school reached higher educational standards by a given age than did a similar groups from a single-sex school. Such a result might well be valid in the statistical sense; and such results could be used justifiably as the basis for educational planning and policy. But such a research project would tell us relatively little about the 'social' (as opposed to the educational) value of the two types of school. Moreover, unlike the physical sciences, such a project as this cannot be used to argue from the general to the particular. In other words, such a result would enable us to say that children in general would do better in a particular educational setting. But we could not say that an individual child would inevitably benefit in such a way since many individual variables will also affect the issue.

Similar problems and difficulties arise when we come to study the family and its relationships with the outside cultural and social environment in which it exists. Here, too, the possible individual variations are almost infinite.

If we study only one family, we can see how very different it is on different occasions. When away on summer holiday it is scarcely the same as on a cold, bleak Monday morning. Summer and winter, morning and evening, working days and weekends, its pattern changes. There are good days and bad days, not only for individual members, but for the family as a whole. One person's mood (even if that person is a small baby) can change the emotional atmosphere for everyone. Even the progress of a single day may have its varying acts and scenes, comedy, farce, thriller or even tragedy, with light relief, moments of tension, denouements, surprise, humour, mystery, drama, exits and entrances, throw away and curtain lines. To continue the metaphor, each member of the family may be called upon to play many parts.

But moving beyond this very simple level of variability, is it possible for us to define what a family is, let alone if there is such a concept as *the* family?

Although considerable variations can (and do) occur in the form, size, role and duration of the family in anthropologically differing settings, the 'family' has been the basic unit of society in most modern and historical civilizations. There are, of course, basic biological and reality factors which explain this frequent appearance of the family unit. Every child must be born to a mother; and that mother or some substitute for her must nurture and care for him during the long period of physical and social dependence which every human child must face. Since the actual survival of any society depends eventually on this new generation, that society must provide some protective support for the pregnant and nursing mother; and it must concern itself with the methods whereby the new generation will be trained to accept their role in the society, and the society's role towards them. Inevitably, therefore, the family (in whatever exact form it appears) will be one of the most powerful and influential features in the society; and a feature which the society will tend to venerate and preserve. Consequently strong conventions and taboos can build up around the role of the family and around the relationships within the family and between the family and the wider society.

Nevertheless, even these established and traditional patterns do change, usually very slowly, but sometimes quite swiftly, in the face of altering cultural needs and pressures; and in their turn these changes in family roles and structures will have their own impact on the general cultural pattern.

It would be outside the scope of this book to study these phenomena in any detail,[1] and one example will suffice here. In Britain the relative roles of husband and father and wife and mother within the family had been long established and accepted. In practice the man was always the wage-earner and provider, and the arbiter on all material or financial policy decisions. In law he was (until comparatively recently) the legal owner of all the family property and the master of the household. By contrast the role of wife and mother was essentially within, and as a part of that household. It was for her to bring up the children, subject to the ultimate authority of the father, and to minister to the family's general welfare. Gradual inroads were made into this stabilized pattern; but within comparatively recent times there have been massive, and relatively rapid changes. Both parents now may well be wage earners,

[1] The reader who wishes to go further will find an interesting and stimulating example of such an anthropological study of modern American society in Dr Margaret Mead's *Male and Female*. Victor Gollancz, London.

both parents may be equally involved in domestic tasks and in the upbringing of the children.

It is not a question of which system is the better. The importance lies in the implications of such changes of role for all concerned; and in the uncertainty and unsureness over these new relative roles within the family which such a change must provoke. Each marriage partner may feel threatened by, or pleased by, his or her new role. It may well conflict with his fantasy picture of the ideal husband or wife, since such fantasy concepts will be partly based at least on past personal or cultural experiences. Such changes will require adjustment in spheres as widely different as (say) the basic concepts of masculinity and feminity or over decisions as to who pays for what in the general household budget. Moreover, as we have seen in earlier chapters, much of the value of the parental role vis-à-vis the child lies in the maturity and confidence with which the adult approaches this task; and the 'genuine' image of motherhood or fatherhood which that adult can provide. Any uncertainty over this role or image, must have obvious and powerful repercussions on the children.

If it is within the framework of the family that we normally develop and discover our individuality, it is also within that same framework that we discover how inevitably the individual is integrated with his environment; and how closely his own actions and feelings interact with those of other people who are close to him.

Although the concept is a somewhat oversimplified one, it may help our understanding of this complex problem if we picture the family as functioning in three separate, but closely inter-related 'layers'.

Every family must consist of a basic 'layer' of individual and separate people. Each will be a different person. Each will have his, or her, own personality built up (as we have tried to describe in this book) from the combination of his past environment, experience and his constitutional make up. According to sex and age and maturity level, the place of each and his role in the family and in the outside world will be different. And, as we have seen, their reactions, feelings and defences will vary from situation to situation; from moment to moment as well as from year to year. The first thing that matters about the family as a whole, then, is the manner of people who form it.

But all these individuals live together as one social unit, with all the dynamic meaning that these words 'live' and 'social unit' can imply. Thus we can see the second layer of family function as the interaction between its individual members. It is easy to say that each member of the family has his role to play; but, as we have seen, these roles vary from moment to moment. Mother, within the course of a few hours, may have to be comforter, arbitrator in a complex rivalry situation between two of the children (and industrial disputes have nothing on such normal family rivalries in terms of complexity of problems or emotional involvement by both sides), adviser on the intricacies of logarithms for her grammar school son, hostess to an entirely unexpected visitor or disciplinary figure. She must know intuitively and confidently which role she must adopt in each quickly changing situation, and carry this role through successfully, despite the knowledge that the milkman is long overdue that morning, or that the joint will be ruined if it is not taken out of the oven immediately. Her dual role as mother and wife may sometimes be, and quite often seem to be, in rivalry with her role as a wife. The fact that the baby kept her awake all last night (to say nothing of the fact that her husband slept through the whole crisis!) or that Johnnie is being provocatively naughty, must influence how this mother will respond not only to Johnnie, her baby and to her husband, but how she responds to all the other situations of the daily round. In turn the other members of her family will respond to her mood and reactions—and the whole pattern of the situation and emotional pattern of the family has changed again.

We have concentrated more on the mother since it is she who is most usually in intimate contact with the family during the day. But when father comes home in the evening and during the week-ends, another new family situation arises and the pattern again changes. He comes into the complex situation as a fresh figure; and whether he is an uninterested, or a demanding father or one who is a very real part of the family, everyone's relationships have to adjust to this new figure. Do the children switch their demands or their overt affection onto him? And does he attack his wife's role by immediately giving way to demands which she has refused, or by manipulating the show of affection (real or otherwise) to his own advantage? At the other extreme does he take over the whole authority and responsibility of the household as soon as he enters the door with his wife gladly, or unwillingly, accepting this change? Or does he come in as an equal member of a partnership bearing in mind that a partnership has been defined as 'the working together of two or more people who each contribute equally according to their means and who share the risks and profits'? All these and many other alternatives are possible. And each will have an entirely different and vital impact not only on the role of father in, and his relationship with, the family but also on all the inter personal relationships of all the members of the family. Moreover this impact is not just at the moment of father's return to the house, or even confined to when he is present in the house. It will affect the family pattern and reactions and all their relationships at other times also.

Nor is it only the parental attitudes which are significant. Some rivalries and jealousy are normal, and indeed, necessary between the children of even the most closely united family. There must be many good and normal parents who have some slight preference for one of their children over the others, however carefully (and usually guiltily) this is covered up. But what of the family situation where such parental preference is openly and powerfully shown? Or where some unavoidable factors accentuate the rivalry between the children; where one is much more intelligent, or duller or more successfully demanding than the others? Or where one child is the 'baby' of a family of grown up brothers and sisters, or the one boy (or girl) in a large family all of the other sex? The rest of the family *must* react to such situations whether they do this constructively or destructively; and new tensions, new feelings and new patterns of relationship must follow to influence not only the present pattern of that family but the individual future of all its members.

Although we may rightly see the family as the basic social unit and the arena where the fortunate majority of us have our first experience of human relationships and begin our social development, the family exists as an integral part of a larger environment. Its third 'layer' of functioning is its interaction with this bigger outside environment.

Father, when he came home in the evening in our illustration already quoted, had come back from work. To say nothing of the frustrations of the traffic jam on his homeward journey, or the opportunity that the railway journey gave him to boast to his friends in the compartment about his prowess at golf the previous week-end, there all the situations of the working day and the relationship patterns at work to have had their impact on him. Does he enjoy his work or find it constantly frustrating; was the boss being difficult and demanding? Or, at a deeper level, what are his feelings about the authority pattern at work (whether he be boss or employee), and how does this contrast or compare with the father-and-husband-roles which he visualizes for himself at home?

Mary has been at school all day, in a social setting that is quite separate from (and different from) home. Her relationship experience at school, the different expectations and interests, whether she had a difficult or easy time with lessons, will all re-appear in her relationships within the family.

The mother may have been at home all day and on her own. Her desperate need may be for some adequate contact with that outside world. Or she, too, may have had a frustrating day of shopping or been at an interesting tea-party with her friends. Whichever it has been, it will influence her reactions as a mother and a wife.

There is, too, the family contact as a whole with the neighbourhood community. Here we can see especially the impact of two major social phenomena of recent years. By comparison there is now far greater mobility both geographically and through the various social and economic levels of society. It is far more common nowadays for the young family to move to new areas; and with this to move away from the security of the area which they have known, and away, too, from their friends and from those parents and in-laws to whom they can turn, however ambivalent their basic feelings may be in that direction. It may be difficult to find in the new setting supportive figures or substitutes for the 'larger family' which they have left behind. It may be difficult for the family even to find new friends or 'fit in' with the new environment. Or to compete with the new standards and expectations if the move has been into a very different social setting from the one in which they grew up. Nor is this the problem of the family only; it will have its repercussions within that family and upon every one of its members.

Since, in this chapter, we have been concerned with the family as a social unit, we have described, and concentrated upon, what are largely reality factors. Even reality factors, as we have seen, will have widespread emotional consequences and produce widespread effects on the reactions, relationships and personalities of those concerned. But, as we have stressed throughout this book, unconscious factors colour much of what we do, or think, or feel. There is always the contrast and comparison between the family as it actually is (and our actual role in it) and that fantasy concept of the family and our role which we have built up as a result of our total life experience and the consequent and largely unconscious conflicts.

The lesson of all this must be that we can only understand (and therefore help) an individual, and we can only understand the development of his personality if we study him both as a 'complete' person and in relationship with his whole environment, past and present. The 'here-and-now' of present events is important; but so are the manner of person that he is and his ability (or inability) to react to that 'here-and-now'.

Conclusion

The purist who has read this far could complain that, both in the title of this book and in its contents, we have misused the word 'personality'. It is perfectly true that personality has not been equated solely with the strength (or weakness) of the ego as a good many psychotherapists and case-workers might wish. At the other extreme, such concepts as character and temperament have been included in our picture of personality, although there are, in terms of strict psychological definition, subtle but important differences between these various terms.

This choice of a much broader definition of personality is deliberate, however, for it was felt that it could contribute more to an understanding of the problem if we regarded personality as meaning 'the total person as he appears to the outside world'. (It is for this reason that 'personality' is used in the actual title of the book, and not 'the personality'.)

What we have tried to do, therefore, is to trace the development of this 'whole person in relationship to his total environment', from the stage when he is completely dependent, to the stage when he can, in every sense of the phrase, 'stand on his own feet'.

It is tempting to say here that we have tried to describe his growth from earliest infancy to maturity. But maturity is another term which we must consider with care.

It is true that, by good interview technique or through suitable projective-type tests, one can make a reasonably accurate assessment of the maturity level of an individual. But maturity is an entirely relative term. We can speak with complete justice of a two-year old being completely mature—for a two-year old. And what may represent immaturity at a given age in one cultural environment might represent an adequate level of maturation at the same age range in a different setting.

What can we do with reasonable certainty, however, is to

describe certain patterns of behaviour as being immature (or over-mature) for a particular individual within a particular social culture. (In this connection, it is worth remembering that, although it may produce fewer immediate problems, over-maturity can produce equally damaging long-term results for the individual as can immaturity.)

Let us consider the following patterns of human behaviour; the inability to accept and cope with the necessary frustration and control; an excessive drive to gratify one's own desires immediately and without regard to the needs of others; a too demanding or too possessive relationship with others; an inability to foresee (or accept) the consequences of one's own action; and thereby an unwillingness to plan ahead.

Whilst such reaction patterns could well arise from other forms of emotional disturbance, these could well be the product of an immature character and/or personality; or, to put it another way, these could be the visible signs of that immaturity.

It is easy to regard such behaviour as only representing moral faults. But it is even more dangerously easy to deny the fact (and the consequences that must follow from this) that reactions of this sort *must* have social and moral implications in any ordered community. We need to remember always the shrewd dictum of the late Lord Birkett that 'to explain human behaviour is not always to excuse it'; and the equally important fact that mature freedom includes the ability to cope with and accept necessary controls and authority. We cannot, for example, entirely equate juvenile delinquency with maladjustment. The two concepts overlap to a considerable degree. But if we regard all juvenile delinquency as an illness, and as the product of emotional disturbances, and if we ignore the character defect (and thus inevitably the moral) aspects of such behaviour we shall fail to help most young delinquents.

This does not mean, of course, that in our consideration of such moral aspects we condemn the individual in terms of a refusal to help him because he is 'bad'. But such considerations remind us that, in the real interest of the individual with a character or personality defect, the total armoury of our treatment facilities must include techniques of social training. Such training in turn must include certain ultimate sanctions, as well as such concepts as disapproval and guilt.

Equally the ability to help must include the techniques of counselling, case-work, psychotherapy and the like used in each case by suitably trained personnel.

Part, at least, of our skills must therefore involve the ability to decide what form of help is the appropriate one in any given situation. To oversimplify the problem, is our aim in any instance to train or to treat?

It is not suggested that this book alone will provide the whole solution to this dilemna; nor that it will alone develop such skills of differential judgement. But what we have tried to do is to evaluate the balance during the process of human development between such opposing (but equally important) factors as freedom and control, conscious decisions and unconscious influences, the give and take of human relationships, parental (and later society's) approval and disapproval, and the need for both dependence on and independence from others.

Only by an understanding of this complex balance and the relative significance of these opposing forces in our growth, and in any specific circumstance, can we hope to help our client by the means most appropriate to him, and to his problem.

This is, basically, the reason and the excuse for this book. For, in the ultimate issue, we must be able to balance theory against the reality of practice; and understand how these apparently opposing factors are, in fact, closely inter-related.

GEORGE ALLEN & UNWIN LTD

London: 40 Museum Street, W.C.1

Auckland: P.O. Box 36013, Northcote Central. N.4
Bombay: 15 Graham Road, Ballard Estate, Bombay 1
Barbados: P.O. Box 222, Bridgetown
Buenos Aires: Escritorio 454-459, Florida 165
Calcutta: 17 Chittaranjan Avenue, Calcutta 13
Cape Town: 68 Shortmarket Street
Hong Kong: 105 Wing On Mansion, 26 Hancow Road, Kowloon
Ibadan: P.O. Box 62
Karachi: Karachi Chambers, McLeod Road
Madras: Mohan Mansions, 38c Mount Road, Madras 6
Mexico: Villalongin 32-10, Piso, Mexico 5, D.F.
Nairobi: P.O. Box 4536
New Delhi: 13-14 Asaf Ali Road, New Delhi 1
Ontario: 81 Curlew Drive, Don Mills
Rio de Janeiro: Caixa Postal 2537-Zc-00
São Paulo: Caixa Postal 8675
Singapore: 36c Prinsep Street, Singapore 7
Sydney, N.S.W.: Bradbury House, 55 York Street
Tokyo: P.O. Box 26, Kamata

Depth Psychology

DIETER WYSS

This book by Dr Dieter Wyss, a practising psychiatrist and psychotherapist in Frankfurt am Main, does not belie its title. It provides both a history and a critique of Depth Psychology. Nor is the historical survey restricted to an account of 'Freud, Adler, Jung'. On the contrary, it systematically pursues the development in this field – in Europe, England and America – from their origins in Freud's predecessors right through to the present day. Dr Wyss presents his material both chronologically under the different schools of depth psychology and thematically in terms of psychological concepts. The result is not only a book of reference but of cross-reference, to which the student of depth psychology may turn both for factual information and comparative assessments over his entire field.

The critical aspect of this work is quite simply an attempt to establish the position of depth psychology today, seventy years after its inception. During those seventy years the field has widened beyond recognition, so that today we are faced with a perplexity of viewpoints, all related to the same endeavour, but all divergent within themselves. Dr Wyss analyses these different attitudes, isolates the problems attendant on each and, on the basis of his analysis, indicates the direction in which further progress in depth psychology might reasonably be expected to lie.

Your Mind Can Heal You

FREDERICK W. BAILES

There is a definite law of mental healing, and that this law can be applied to anyone, regardless of his mental strength or will-power, is conclusively demonstrated in this inspiring book. It is a practical introduction to the technique of mental and physical treatment. It is compatible with every religious belief; actually it is scientific rather than religious.

While a student at a large London hospital, Dr Bailes closely observed the mental factors which entered into the recovery of patients. During the subsequent years he proved conclusively that both sickness and health find their origin in corresponding mental states, that there is a definite technique of mental and spiritual treatment which sets mental law in action and as a result brings physical health.

GEORGE ALLEN & UNWIN LTD